i

Pain is a Stimulus

Pain is a Stimulus

Strength by Necessity

ShoMari Payne

Independently Published

ISBN - 13:
978-1091799219

I would like to dedicate this book to my late Grandfather, Curtis W. Payne Sr.

Contents

Forward

As a Certified Strength Conditioning Specialist (CSCS) my primary mission is to help individuals improve their physical performance through exercise prescription. Originally, I sought to write a book filled with workout plans, functional exercises with detailed illustrations, coupled with sound wellness advice. Somewhere along the line, I decided to evolve this project to impact the mind and the body. I believe exercise is God's gift to humanity; an overlooked analogy that teaches us how discipline, consistency, vision, and pushing through temporary pain and discomfort can transform physical circumstances. I realized that I was ready to share my unique experience with poverty, and my continuous journey of self-development. I was ready to reveal where I found the switch to activate my own innate power to endure tough times, and manifest brighter days; a power that resides within us all. While writing and rewriting this book I became motivated to empower the spirit of impoverished communities, school districts, families, and individuals. Writing this book has been infinitely therapeutic, and divinely necessary for my personal growth and continuing evolution in thought. I pray that it may provide such a benefit along your own unique journey. *Pain is a Stimulus* is filled with stories, poems, and life experiences, some victories, and many defeats. Join me on a journey that began when I was five months old.

You must go through pain in order to become you

Competitive Advantage

I have forever been fascinated with the science of exercise, better known as "exercise science." Like most young African-American boys that grew up during the 90's, I loved basketball. For as long as I can remember, I invested massive amounts of energy into the strength and conditioning aspect of sports. I made this commitment in hopes of jumping higher, running faster, and becoming physically stronger. My hope was that this investment would result in a competitive advantage on the basketball court. Most days, I completed hundreds of calf-raises during idle times and rattled off endless sets of sit-ups on the living room floor. When I needed some resistance, I would walk up the street and bench press those old school sanded weights on a wobbly bench in my friend Nic Bean's backyard. But most importantly, I was always dribbling my cheap rubber basketball throughout my neighborhood for hours on end, beneath the streetlights. I had enlisted in the ranks, joining thousands of other African-American young men embarking on the quest for basketball greatness. Along my journey, I stumbled upon the concept of explosive jump training, and it immediately consumed me. I loved the notion that through consistent effort and an advanced understanding of human performance, I could tilt the odds of athleticism in my favor. Each of us are born with two types of skeletal muscle fibers, slow-twitch (type I) and fast-twitch (type II). Slow-twitch muscles help sustain long-endurance feats such as distance running, marathons, and swimming, while fast-twitch muscles fatigue more quickly but are used in powerful bursts of movements like sprinting, accelerating, and explosive jumping.

hops aka bounce
: excessive vertical, the ability to jump very high, preferably in a hoop game

I never had a father in the household to teach me how to play sports or lift weights, nor a mother willing to sacrifice her time and money to send me off to basketball camps during the summer. So I concluded early on, that if I could just jump higher than everyone else, I had a solid chance to not only make the basketball team, but maybe make it to the Pros. In my city, Dayton, Ohio, a high vertical jump (aka bounce or hops) was an elusive tool that held the power to catapult you out of your impoverished neighborhood, and land you on the doorstep of a thriving college campus. Your bounce was the secret weapon that could transform you from no-name, to mainstream after just one viral dunk. Around this time, a kid named Romain Sato held the keys to bounce in my city. Romain was a freakishly athletic, 6'4 guard who played varsity basketball for Dayton Christian High School. I remember attending one of his high school games as a 7th grader with my friends Mario and Aaron. Romain was playing against our future high school, Jefferson. I remember the game like it was yesterday, and even during the warm-ups, I was completely mesmerized by his superior athleticism. From the opening tip, he picked up right where he left off during the layup line, with a monstrous dunk followed by an alley-oop flush, and then a jaw-dropping acrobatic layup over two defenders. I was a 5'6 pipsqueak, so all the guys at my future high school were giants to me, but Romain was my first glimpse of elite athleticism. His athletic prowess landed him on the prestigious campus of Xavier University in Cincinnati, Ohio, and eventually to a small stint in the NBA. I wanted to go up to him after the game and inquire about his training regimen, but this would have been the equivalent of attempting to get next to LeBron James in 2003, following a St. Vincent St. Mary high school game. Nonetheless, I doubt he would have been willing to reveal his blueprint, even if I was able to steal a minute of his time.

After watching Romain Sato at that Dayton Christian game, I was determined to get my hands on a pair of 10 lb. sanded ankle weights. At least once a week I would catch the RTA (city bus) from my Grandma's house in Jefferson Township to MC Sports (MC) in Trotwood, Ohio, just to stare at them. I was convinced that after just a few weeks of training with the ankle weights, I would be jumping out of the gym just like Romain, and I'd be virtually unstoppable. I imagined the scholarship letters would be pouring in faster than I could keep up with. Once while at MC, I contemplated stealing them, but I determined they were too heavy to conceal. Eventually, my Grandpa Payne purchased the ankle weights for me, but after weeks of walking around my neighborhood with those bulky weights strapped to me ankles, I was unable to jump any higher. A few months passed and one day while reading SLAM magazine, a miracle fell from the Heavens (SLAM is a popular basketball publication that every basketball junkie read to pass the time). The back pages of every SLAM magazine were dedicated to new advertisements, and this is where I stumbled upon the phenomena of strength shoes. Strength shoes were ginormous platform-shoes that forced you to walk on the balls of your feet. You would keep your regular shoes on, slide your feet inside the strength shoes, tighten the strap, and walk around until your calves were fatigued. The science behind the product was simple: bigger calves equated to more athletic explosion. There were several variations and brands of strength shoes, and on my fourteenth birthday, Grandpa Payne ordered me a pair of Jumpsoles. Anyone who played basketball in the late 90's and early 2000's wanted a pair; I know because some kid stole mine at an open gym a few months later. Here is their ad below.

Did you know that, when you wear regular athletic shoes, about 70% of your weight lands on your heels? Changing the distribution of your body weight during training is the key to the unique design of our shoes. By eliminating the heel, our strength training shoes force you to stand on the balls of your feet, fully engaging your calves.

Strength Shoes Advertisement

"What 13-year-old couldn't be enthralled with the promise of 'Increase your vertical jump by 10-12 inches' To a young athlete, it was like these words were proclaimed from the heavens, calling forth all those wanting to embark on a sacred journey to defy gravity. How could this not be true?"

Joel Smith, M.S, CSCS

I still remember the day they arrived in the mail, I ripped open the box, nestled my feet inside, tightened the Velcro strap, and walked around my neighborhood for hours. When I finished walking, my calves were bloodshot red, but I knew this was the necessary sacrifice to improve my vertical jump. After a few months of wearing Jumpsoles, I concluded that they helped increase the physical size of my calf muscles, but they didn't improve my jumping ability like the ad had guaranteed. So here I was, disappointed by a second failed attempt at improving my bounce, and started feeling the pressure of my proverbial basketball window steadily closing. A few years later, I saw another ad in the back of SLAM for a promising vertical jump program called "Air Alert." Air Alert was endorsed by NBA players Larry Hughes and Baron Davis, neither of whom were extraordinary leapers, but they both had pulled off some rather impressive dunks from time to time. I figured Air Alert was worth a shot and pleaded with Grandpa Payne for another $50 investment; he reluctantly agreed. Air Alert consisted of 5 different jumping movements: Leap-Ups, Calf-Raises, Thrust-Ups, Step-Ups, and Burnouts. The repetitions became increasingly difficult every week, but the progressive science of the program sold me on its potential to increase my athleticism.

AIR ALERT ADVANCED											
	Step ups		Leap ups		Burnouts		Leap ups		Burnouts		Thrust ups	
	Sets	Reps	Sets	Reps	Sets	Reps	Sets	Reps	Sets	Reps	Sets	Reps
1	1	15	3	15	1	100	3	15	1	100	1	20
3	1	20	3	20	1	150	3	20	1	150	1	25
5	1	20	3	20	1	175	3	20	1	175	1	30
2	1	15	3	15	1	125	3	15	1	125	1	20
4	1	20	3	20	1	150	3	20	1	150	1	25
6	1	25	3	25	1	175	3	25	1	175	1	30

Image of the Air Alert Training Protocol

By this time, my understanding of the vertical jump had at least evolved to a level where I realized that the physical act of jumping was a better method for improving my vertical jump than simply walking around on my toes in some ridiculous shoes. Air Alert was literally a step in the right direction, but still fail vastly short in respect to the scientific information that was available during that era to improve my sports performance. Today, I have a much deeper understanding of scientific training principles like the French contrast method, bi-lateral force deficit, and post-activation potentiation, all of which are proven methods for progressively improving the vertical jump. I squandered many resources before realizing that a strength and conditioning book would have been my best initial investment, instead of falling victim to the clever marketing advertisements of the Strength Shoe, Jumpsoles, ankle weights, and Air Alert.

INFORMATION CHANGES SITUATIONS

"We must educate our children early, with the information that came to us late"
Rashard Cartwright

The information in this book has the potential to alter the trajectory of your life, enlighten the darkness of your perspective, and inspire you to abandon expired habits. Many stories and principles outlined in this book are a bridge between human performance and mental visualization, bringing these two inseparable sciences together to discover intrinsic motivation and manifestation. The mind and the body cannot be divided, and when we attempt to divide the two we impose a grave injustice on ourselves. In my life, I have used these sciences to become the embodying proof that to overcome insurmountable odds you must remain faithful to one overarching principle, YOU MUST NOT QUIT! For nearly two decades, I wrestled with adversity, slept with poverty, struggled with depression, and above all, accepted defeat. My opponent seemed immovable, and I felt powerless in my ability to alter my circumstances. In the following chapters, I will share more of my story and the stories of others, as I attempt to solder the science of human performance and the spirit of persistence, with the power of visualization. Looking back, I have overcome many of the barriers that were present in my life. According to U.S Census income data from 1987, my economic position today would not appear much different than it did during my years in bondage, but my true fortune lies in the wisdom that I forged through necessity. My childhood was defined through my intimate experience with extreme poverty, deliberate oppression, hazardous hoarding, a high-poverty public school district, massive community disinvestment, and deep individual depression. Allow me to share some background statistics with you before we begin our journey.

Oppressive Poverty

"Poverty is hunger. Poverty is a lack of shelter. Poverty is being sick and not being able to see a doctor. Poverty has many faces"

World Bank Association

relative poverty - occurs when people do not enjoy a certain minimum level of living standards as determined by the government (and enjoyed by the bulk of population).

oppression - prolonged cruel or unjust treatment or exercise of authority.

U.S Census Data - 1987

1) In 1987, the U.S median family income was $30,850, a 1% increase from 1986.

2) The median income of families with a female householder, no husband present, increased from $14,146 in 1986 to $14,620 in 1987, a 3.4% increase; this is the 2nd significant annual increase since 1979.

3) In 1987, 10.5% of Whites were in poverty, a decrease of .5% from 1986; 33.1% of Blacks were in poverty, an increase of 2%.

Dayton, Ohio
(Present Day)

In the Dayton area, about 62.8 percent of the population lives predominantly in neighborhoods of their own races. Below is some recent demographic data on Dayton, Ohio from *24/7 Wall St.*
(24/7 is a financial news Web site that covers the stock market, industry research and government policy bearing on the economy).

1. Black people in black neighborhoods: 29.6%

2. Black population: 15.4%

3. Black poverty rate: 34.1%

4. White poverty rate: 12.6%

"The more things change, the more they stay the same"
Jean-Baptiste Alphonse Karr

Poverty and oppression were the common denominators in my upbringing. I was raised solely by my Grandmother in a home that was hazardously hoarded on the westside of Dayton, Ohio in a neighborhood called Jefferson Township. Grandma received around $800.00 monthly by way of a social security check, and she never obtained her driver's license. This lack of income combined with our immobility added to our disenfranchisement. She also earned a couple hundred dollars a month as a foot soldier delivering the Dayton Daily Newspaper. By the time I entered the second grade, Grandma had retired from delivering the newspaper, and was no longer receiving this much needed part-time wage. Some of my earliest memories involve us trekking up and down our neighborhood streets tossing these massive newspapers, wrapped in blue plastic, into a thick morning fog. The papers that Grandma pitched always landed precisely on the doorstep of the recipient, mine oftentimes fell embarrassingly short, and I'd have to pick it up and place it on the porch. Grandma stands around 5'10, but to me she was seven feet tall, strong and poised like all of the older black people I knew that migrated from the south. Every morning she'd wake me up, and I reluctantly helped her package and deliver the newspapers before I went to school. During our paper route morning runs, I'd constantly complain about the intense walking, and she would immediately refer me to her own humble beginnings, "Me and my sisters walked ten miles to school on dirt roads with plastic bags for shoes." My frustration would immediately shift to inquisition, as I was always intrigued by her experience growing up in the South during the apex of Jim Crow; it was those conversations that sparked my lifelong obsession with race relations in America. "Did you ever see the KKK," I would ask, "Yep, and I wudnt scared of em either," she'd always respond.

To navigate around the city, we relied primarily on the Regional Transit Authority (RTA), the city of Dayton's public transportation system. We'd hop on the RTA to pay the DP&L (Dayton Power & Light), Vectren (Gas company), pick up the few groceries we could afford, and sometimes just to escape our home environment for a few hours.

xvii

Grandma barely had enough for the bills, let alone anything extra, but she always tried to save a few dollars so I could purchase a treat during school lunch. Every night, we both went to bed hungry, and took turns sleeping on the floor. "But you had the couch last night Grandma," I'd exclaim, she would usually laugh and say, "Ok ShoMari," then trade me spots for the night. Many nights I felt guilty looking down from the couch and watching Grandma struggle attempting to find comfort on the floor, but it was the system of equity that we had set up to survive. Soon I quit requesting the couch, as I saw how the floor was affecting her back and her walk, and I accepted the floor full-time. During the summer months we circulated contaminated air from cheap electric fans, and our humble space heaters were no match for the frigid Ohio winters. But the worst part of our life was my mom, although she did not physically stay with us, a large part of her did, and it profoundly affected how Grandma and I survived.

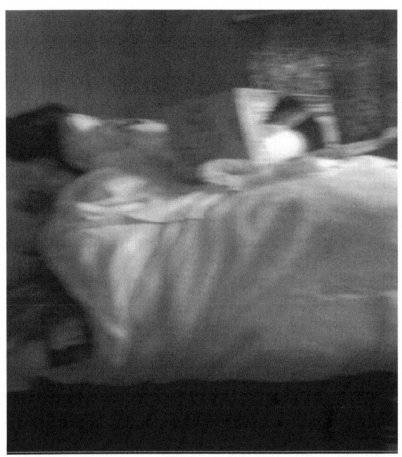

Kitchen table

Hoarding

Below is an excerpt from a study completed by the Metropolitan Boston Housing Partnership.

In the United States, approximately 15 million people (3-5 percent of the population) suffer from hoarding disorder. Hoarding can be more about fear of throwing something away than about collection or saving. Thinking about discarding an item triggers anxiety in the hoarder, so they hang on to the item to prevent anxiety. In a study on hoarding, it was determined that family members rated the person who hoards as having limited insight into the severity of their hoarding, and more than half described the person as either having poor or no insight. People who lived with a person who hoards during their childhood years reported being significantly more embarrassed about their home, having fewer visitors, experiencing more strain in their relationship with their parents, and having an unhappier childhood than did people who did not grow up in a hoarding home. Most family members reported arguing with the person who hoards about the problem at least somewhat. They also studied family attitudes toward the person who hoards. Scores on a measure of family frustration equaled or exceeded those found for family members of hospitalized patients with schizophrenia in previous studies. Not surprisingly, more family frustration was significantly associated with poorer insight on the part of the person who hoards. These results show us that living with hoarding has adverse effects on the quality of the family relationships.

Metropolitan Boston Housing Partnership

The hoarding I experienced was ironic because the primary hoarder was not physically present in the home. However, she managed to transform a 1,200 sq. ft house into a complete dumping ground, a dark desolate place overrun with rats and cockroaches. A place where she could leave the things she wasn't ready to completely throw away or destroy, including myself and her mother. My mom (who I will often refer to as Gloria, which is more comfortable for me) lived with her boyfriend, 10-15 minutes north of us, but it felt as though an ocean were between us. She was largely inaccessible, and as I mentioned, Grandma never obtained her driver's license. We were in some ways her slaves, her abandoned refugees, desperately hoping she might stop by to drop off some bottled water or canned food that couldn't be penetrated by the roaches. Grandma and I felt as though we were being punished for a crime that we did not commit, "Tell her she has to get her stuff out of here Grandma; this is your house," I would plead. I owe my sense of logic today to those heated discussions with Grandma regarding the culprit of our oppression. Some days Grandma would see things from my perspective and confront her daughter, "Gloria, ShoMari has a point, I'm a need you to get your stuff out of here." Other days, her love for her first-born was no match for even my best counter-arguments.

"In the 2015 Metropolitan Boston Housing Partnership conducted an intervention study on Hoarding. The most common factor among hoarders, was at 33 percent with garbage/trash overflow, followed by an inability to sleep in their bed."

Metropolitan Boston Housing Partnership

My newfound backbone would cause Gloria to disappear for months at a time, which was a subtle reminder that she possessed the only driver's license between the three of us, and without her, we were slaves to the schedule of the #22 RTA bus. The #22 was a lifeline, our consistent transportation to the grocery store, doctor appointments, to pay the Dayton Power & Light, and run all of Grandma's other errands. On the rare occasions Gloria stopped by our roach-infested home, she would frantically and compulsively examine all of the bedrooms to ensure none of her belongings had been altered or disposed of. "Who been in my room," she would yell, "I had this stuff organized." It was an intense workout to pry open bedroom doors, climb through stockpiles of old clothes, and inhale the stench from old paper plates. Gloria is the oldest of Grandma's three biological children, and she could never do wrong in Grandma's eyes. Grandma graciously accepted her position on our old, defeated brown couch, the kind that you see sitting next to a dumpster in low-income apartment complexes. It was there where an aging migrant from the South was forced to sleep after overcoming decades of discrimination, segregation, oppression, and racism, in the twilight of her golden years. She accepted this final dance with oppression in her own home, while Gloria enjoyed the luxuries of her newfound relationship, along with the surplus of a child support stipend from my father. The hoarding turned a three-bedroom house into a roach and rat-infested kitchen, unsanitary bathroom, and three garbage-filled, inaccessible bedrooms. Grandma and I shared a small section in the living room where we were forced to spend all of our time. No childhood friend ever stepped foot inside my home.

Depression

"Depression is a common but serious mood disorder. It causes severe symptoms that affect how you feel, think, and handle daily activities, such as sleeping, eating, or working. To be diagnosed with depression, the symptoms must be present for at least two weeks"

National Institute of Mental Health

My bout with depression began early in childhood, around the second grade, and lasted until the day I left for college. I was depressed about sleeping on the floor, about the infestation of roaches and mice, about not being able to invite friends over, with how Gloria treated Grandma and I, and with my existence altogether. Many days I contemplated disclosing my living conditions to teachers, counselors, police, other family members, or children's services, but ultimately, I opted to protect the family secret. I was too embarrassed by what the potential ridicule or publicity might look like. I often envisioned my house being the subject of the evening news, my story paraded throughout the Dayton Daily Newspaper, and I decided early on that it wasn't worth the embarrassment. During this decade of depression, I picked up countless habits that would take years to identify and discard. I was never diagnosed with clinical depression (because I was never taken to the doctor), but one glimpse into my circumstances from an outsider would have resulted in no other conclusion. During my early teenage years, I contemplated suicide once again, but I ultimately opted to bury the pain back inside myself. School was always rough; I hated going because I was routinely picked on for circumstances that were beyond my control. I wanted to have great hygiene, but Grandma had trouble keeping up with the water bill, let alone stockpiling toothpaste and deodorant. Early in my youthful ignorance, I genuinely wanted to invite friends over, but I feared the backlash and embarrassment from revealing my living situation. Even if I had the courage to do so, or trusted a friend with such a heavy secret, it was an unwritten but understood rule that company was forbidden. So, I hid my living conditions as best as I could. "How come nobody ever gets to go in your house," neighborhood parents and friends began to ask. When presented with this question I would defer, deflect, and always say, "My Grandma doesn't like people coming over," or "We're doing some remodeling right now." But my friends soon got clever and would knock on the door and request me to come out to play, and while standing on the porch ask my Grandma, "Mrs. Clark can I use the restroom, I have to go really bad," she would kindly respond, "I'm sorry baby our restroom isn't working." I learned to meet friends outside before they even got to our falling fence, so there would be no opportunity for shenanigans. I was exclusively known as the kid in the neighborhood who wasn't allowed to have company. It didn't matter if there was a Tornado Warning and you were locked out of your house; you better knock on another door.

Fast forward to high school, I was truant throughout my entire four years. I opted to stay home at our roach palace rather than be heckled by classmates. The daily stress from my home environment coupled with poor nutrition, bad hygiene, and unsanitary living conditions, fueled severe acne breakouts. So instead of facing the collective ridicule from high school comedians, I skipped school; at least the roaches and the rats didn't make fun of me. Teachers habitually told me that I would not graduate, and that I would become another statistic because of my excessive absences and lackluster effort on the rare occasions I did show up. In addition to my adverse environmental conditions, I also suffered from a health condition called Hyperhidrosis. Hyperhidrosis affects around 3% of the global population. Hyperhidrosis is a condition that causes a person to sweat profusely, and my affected area was my hands. I was never taken to a doctor for this condition as a child, and it wasn't until I went to the campus Health Center as a sophomore in college that I was officially diagnosed. This condition affected me socially, academically, emotionally, and athletically. I held less self-confidence than my peers, and I feared social situations that required handshakes. I remember writing lengthy papers for school that would be soaked upon completion, which further fueled my academic frustrations. I would air-ball jump shots that I knew had plenty of mustard on them. I would unintentionally allow golf clubs and bats to slip out of my hands during practice swings and sometimes the club would go flying. Friends at school hated shaking hands with me, I left PlayStation controllers flooded with water-damage, and I couldn't drive without the windows rolled down, so my hands could cool off, or else they'd slip right off the wheel. I'm convinced that my Hyperhidrosis was sparked due to the stress of my home environment. The last piece of my depression was about no longer seeing my Dad. He left Dayton, Ohio in 1996 when the Defense Electronic Supply Center (DESC) government base shut down. At its peak in the 1970s, almost 5,000 military and civilian personnel were employed at DESC. Dad accepted a position at the Defense Supply Center Columbus (DSCC), and moved 70 miles east to Columbus, Ohio.

Our bi-weekly visits were substantially impacted by his relocation. A shining light in my life were his parents; I loved visiting my Grandparent's house. They owned a 3-story home in a suburb of Dayton. Their home was equipped with cable television, a quarter acre of land, a futon in the basement, a refrigerator full of food, and my Grandpa, who was my childhood hero.

ACT I

My childhood was defined by my intimate experience with poverty, hoarding, and depression. As a child I never knew the warmth of a mother's love or the daily discipline instilled by a father. The lion's share of my childhood memories consists of watching my Grandmother deteriorate in our dilapidated home, which was overrun with piles of outdated newspapers, cabinets full of expired canned goods, and rooms packed with mountains of unworn clothes. Every room in the house was filled to the brim and largely inaccessible, forcing Grandma and I to find refuge on the living room floor. Each summer we circulated contaminated air from cheap electric fans filled with brown clots of dust, and every frigid Ohio winter we shivered to the cheap warmth of space heaters and our gas stove. Not only was the house unsanitary due to the extreme hoarding, it was infested with rodents and cockroaches. Every night, I struggled to fall asleep on the floor amid the noise of scurrying rats in the adjacent kitchen. Every morning I'd sprint to the bus stop early, before the other kids arrived, to shake out the fifteen or so cockroaches that nestled inside my backpack overnight, praying the entire way to school that I shook hard enough. I hated sleeping on the floor, but for fifteen straight years that's exactly where I slept. No childhood friend ever stepped foot inside my home. Throughout my childhood I envisioned escaping this toxic environment, all the while desperately trying to keep it a secret.

ACT I chronicles the first few decades of my life, my humble beginnings…

Chapter I
Humble Beginnings

*"They got my 6-year-old nephew in there, he doesn't have any food, and
he sleeping on the floor, they got him living trifling"*
Aunt Rita

*"I remember it was no lights, mattress on the floor, thousand roaches,
four mice, yeah I remember all them cold nights"*
Meek Mill

Dayton, Ohio
September 22, 1987

I was born on September 1987 at Miami Valley Hospital, in downtown
Dayton, Ohio. At this time, my parents were married, and both were
securely employed, placing me into an uncommon circumstance based
upon my demographic profile; the elusive stability of a two parent
African-American home. On the day I entered the world I was
surrounded by infinite love, in large part due to the presence of my four
grandparents: Curtis and Joyce Payne (Dad's side), Arthur & Alice
Clark (Gloria's side). In 1987, my parents were both civilian employees
of the Federal Government, working at the Defense Electronic Supply
Center (DESC) in Kettering, Ohio. Gloria began working for the
government at seventeen, and Dad acquired his civilian contract
following his short stint in the Army around the age of 23. But just as
many other African-American children born during this era, my true
support system resided in the presence of my Grandparents. Grandpa
and Grandma Clark lived in a 3-bedroom house on the westside of
Dayton, the "black-side."

Westown Shopping Center – Dayton, Ohio

My parents also stayed on the westside of Dayton in a small two-bedroom apartment in an inner-suburb called Trotwood, Ohio, an extension of Dayton's black residents. Dad's parents, Curtis Payne Sr. & Joyce Payne, were the most economically successful of the cohort. Grandpa Payne served in the Air Force for over 20 years and Grannie Payne worked for the Federal Aviation Administration (FAA) in the U.S Customs department. The Payne's had two children, my dad (Curtis.Jr), and my Uncle Barry. Both were born in Richmond, Virginia but spent parts of their childhood overseas due to my Grandpa's military obligations. The Payne's eventually settled in Dayton, Ohio by way of Wright Patterson Air Force Base. Grandpa and Grannie Payne built a 3-bedroom home in a quiet suburb just outside of Dayton, in the city of Vandalia, Ohio. Even today, Vandalia has few black residents; according to the 2010 census, the racial makeup of Vandalia was 91.5% white, and only 4.1% black. Vandalia hosts a strong public-school district, and is home to the struggling, but resilient, Dayton International Airport. Back then and still today, obtaining residency status in Vandalia, Ohio was the American Dream for Dayton's black residents.

4

Vandalia, Ohio

My parents married in 1986, the year prior to my birth. On the day I arrived at Miami Valley Hospital, all four of my grandparents were eager to support the newlyweds and their new bundle of joy. Unfortunately for me, things took a sharp turn rather abruptly. By the following May of 1988, my eighth month on earth, the ink on the divorce papers had already dried, and I was headed into a sea of custodial uncertainty. Was I to live with my dad, who had already left a previous marriage and my three older half-siblings in his distant past? Or Gloria, who reluctantly opted not to terminate me, hoping that a baby would be a fresh start to a troubled marriage? Divorces are rarely easy puzzles to solve for either party; but the split was a particularly devastating blow to Gloria. Although they had both been previously married, she had a greater emotional investment in this marriage. I was her first and only child, a last hurrah to salvage a sinking marriage. Gloria feared the reality of a life that included just the two of us.

Following the court proceedings, the State of Ohio awarded full custody to Gloria, along with a guaranteed bi-weekly percentage of my dad's already divided income. In a flash, I was no longer in the familiarity of my marijuana filled apartment in Trotwood, Ohio, and became a resident of the westside of Dayton with Gloria's parents, the Clarks.

Before my 2nd birthday, Gloria had already filled the void of divorce with a full-time boyfriend, whom I will refer to as "Derrick." Derrick worked at one of the largest General Motors plants in the country, which also happened to be the major blue-collar employer for the region. I remember meeting Derrick at the age of two, when he took me, Gloria, and his two sons on a fun-filled adventure to Kings Island (a local amusement park). Derrick scored par with me on that day: he was friendly, bought me ice-cream, and this was my first ever trip to Kings Island. Little did I know this would be the last positive image I'd ever have of him. Gloria swiftly moved in with Derrick and left the full responsibility of raising me with her elderly parents. It happened so fast, I barely noticed that she was gone. Moving forward, I saw her maybe twice a week for thirty or so minutes at a time when she would stop by to check on her belongings that remained at Papa and Grandma Clark's house. To date, Gloria and I have never watched a movie together, never shared a meal at a restaurant or dinner table, never embraced in a hug, and never cultivated any resemblance of a traditional mother-son relationship.

Papa Clark

"And when youth comes to age for advice, he receives the wisdom of years"
George S. Clason

Arthur Clark Jr. "Papa Clark" was Gloria's father, and I lived with him and Grandma Clark immediately following my parents' divorce. I have only a handful of memories of Papa Clark because he passed away when I was only five years old. I know that he was a retired police officer, and a veteran of the U.S Air Force. As I grew older, Uncle Art shared stories with me about Papa, which helped me learn more about his life. He told me that Papa entered the service at 15 years old, he lied about his age so he could enlist. After enlistment he was shipped across the world to fight in the Korean War. Papa almost lost his life in battle; he was gunned down while attempting to carry another soldier to safety. I remember Papa showed me the scars from his gunshot wound during one of our bedside conversations. Following his life-threatening injuries

6

Papa was air-flighted back to the states, where he would recover, learn to write with his opposite hand, and eventually meet his future wife, Alice Davis. From the time I can remember he was bed stricken and very ill. Despite being in constant pain, he would openly share his wisdom with me, and pour into me all the love that he had the strength to muster. He always praised me for my intelligence and would often seem apologetic about how the house was starting to deteriorate. One memory that stands out is the time he surprised me with Toys R Us cash for my birthday, which I used to purchase all four Ninja Turtles action figures. I remember he cried joyously upon witnessing my excitement. I don't remember him ever moving from the bed, and he was always hooked up to IVs, but I do remember his voice, and how loved I felt by him. Another memory that stands out is the day Papa and I were home alone, and he asked me to fetch him some ice for his mug. I was very small, and the freezer was just beyond my reach, so this was no easy task. I walked into the kitchen, pulled up a chair to the freezer, and attempted to remove the semi-frozen ice cubes from the tray. I failed miserably, clumsily dropping the ice tray, and flooding the kitchen floor. I returned to Papa's bedside defeated, "I'm sorry Papa," I immediately saw disappoint engulf his face. This was the last clear memory I have of Papa alive. The final memory I have of Papa was the day I was called to the office at Blairwood elementary school. Grandma was waiting up front and informed me that I was leaving school early so we could visit Papa in the hospital.

I vaguely recall his funeral, but I remember it being a time of extreme sadness for my family. At the time I wasn't fully able to comprehend the magnitude of death, that it was forever. After Papa Clark passed away, Gloria began moving tons of her clothes and other belongings into her recently widowed mother's home. I remember being excited at first, I figured if she was moving her things in, she would soon follow, but she never did. Looking back, it was as if the death of her father was the only thing preventing her from executing the next phase of her life, destroying mine. As they say, misery loves company, and she was truly an unhappy woman. Suddenly, I transitioned from rotating between sleeping on the couch and floor, to being forced to sleep on the floor, in what I was trained to call a pallet. As more and more of her belongings arrived, the occasional roach in the house had reproduced exponentially, and I began seeing them constantly crawling up and down the walls. I remember the home shifting from a place I could frolic and play, into a landmine full of wired hangers, outdated clothes, bags of trash, and rubber maids full of old VHS tapes. I remember Gloria continuously reminding me not to share "family business" when I would visit relatives on my father's side of the family. After Papa Clark passed away my life changed completely. This is when Grandma's house went from a traditional messy and overcrowded home, to being hoarded, and infested with cockroaches and mice.

pallet:
a combination of sheets and blankets placed on the floor for sleeping on.

My pallet

Grandma Clark

Following Papa's passing, Grandma Clark found herself in a peculiar position, coping with the pain of her husband's death, while left with the unwarranted responsibility of raising another child alone in her mid-sixties. I would often catch her crying, but she never explained the root of her tears. Her life of persistence, diligence, and love had landed her the obligation of a second parenthood in her sixties. Around this time, I began asking Grandma questions that she had no desire to answer, "Why do we have so many bugs, my friends don't have bugs at their house." "Grandma how come I don't have a bed; my friend has a bed at his house." I was always obsessed with having a bed, I yearned for one more than anything in the world. Even at five years old I thought sleeping on the floor was the most troubling part of my childhood. For starters that's where the mice and roaches seemed to congregate the most. I was so scared of them, when I saw a mouse scurry across the house I would leap onto the couch and stand there for hours. You could always hear them in the kitchen, which was my warning not to enter for at least a few hours. I also thought the floor was grossly uncomfortable, distinguishably cold, and spatially confining. I knew that we had beds in two of the three rooms, but they were covered with mountains of Gloria's junk and completely inaccessible. Grandma thought my pleas for a more comfortable living environment were hilarious. She was born in Munford, Alabama in 1929, during the height of Jim Crow, so mice, roaches, and sleeping on the floor were no dilemma for such a seasoned warrior. Grandma would always share stories of the southern struggles she and her siblings endured daily. Stories about walking ten miles to school in the Alabama heat with plastic bags for shoes. I remember constantly interrogating her regarding any run-ins with the Ku Klux Klan (KKK). She told me about a time during her adolescence when a few Klansmen attempted to invade her childhood home, but her father was strapped with a shotgun, and prepared for their invasion. I often pondered over the fear she and her siblings must have felt that night, something about the KKK uniforms was always particularly terrifying to me as a child, maybe they weren't to her. She shared these stories with me to teach me that not everyone is born into ideal circumstances, and I was just the latest edition in a long legacy of survivors. The inheritance from a Trans-Atlantic voyage that swallowed many of our ancestors at sea. She wanted me to be grateful, despite being oppressed. Grandma spent her summers watching soap operas, of which All My Children was the only one that I could manage to watch with her. During elementary school Grandma would help me get dressed, remove my unorganized papers from my backpack and shake it outside the front door, and send me off to school with a Flintstone vitamin (which I began to spit out when I was beyond her sight). Some mornings she would cook up a bowl of oatmeal, but I only chose to eat it if I ensured no roaches had crawled on the pot.

"I prayed for twenty years but received no answer, until I prayed with

my legs"

Frederick Douglass

Papa and Grandma Clark had three biological children, in the order of Gloria, Aunt Rita, and Uncle Art. Additionally they raised my Aunt Nancy, the daughter of my Aunt Louise (Grandma's sister). Gloria never got along with any of her three siblings, but they all seemed to embrace me which I truly valued. Aunt Rita, graduated summa cum laude with a bachelor's degree in engineering from Central State University in Wilberforce, Ohio in the early 80's. She is a brilliant woman, giving birth to the first degree to ever emerge from my immediate family. My fondest memories of us involve her randomly quizzing me on math and science, and us playing Sega Genesis together on Grandma's Zenith fatback TV while we sat on my pallet. "ShoMari you need to be careful playing that game, you gon make my picture go out," Grandma would say. We both counted her concerns as just old folk talk and returned to X-Men or Sonic the hedgehog. Somewhere during Aunt Rita's undergraduate days at Central State, she began experimenting with drugs, and this casual hobby transformed into addiction during the late 80's, early 90's. She began to share with me her strange premonitions, like how she was being aggressively followed by key Government officials. Even as a gullible young boy I found her stories farfetched, but I entertained her with smiles and a curious ear. On several occasions she would point to what she claimed were UFOs in the night's sky, but I never saw what she saw. I think part of my disbelief stemmed from the fact that she had hocked my Sega Genesis on several occasions, and she always smelled like cigarettes. In my mind I couldn't understand why the CIA would be stalking a woman who reeked of cigarettes. I remember catching her with my Sega tucked beneath the arm of her long, draping, jet-black leather jacket, "Aunt Rita where you going with the game," I would ask, "I'm just borrowing it baby, don't tell your mom," she would respond. Like any kid pissed by the absence of his 32-bit game console, I snitched, which fueled further disdain from Grandma and Gloria for my Aunt's addiction. After the passing of a few weeks, Aunt Rita would come back over with a new game system for me, and some money. "I told you to trust your Auntie, I got these people following me I had to go get some money, but I will always pay you back nephew." I didn't believe her stories about the CIA following her, but I did believe that she loved me at her core. Before she would depart the house to venture out into her own world, she would always kiss me on the forehead and tell me, "You're not supposed to be living like this nephew, you're a King."

"She even sold da Nintendo, I'm thinking like hol up"
Meek Mill

CHAPTER II
BEDTIME STORY

"My bed was a pallet on the carpet"
2-Chainz

I remember the day Grandma told me not to open the door for Aunt Rita anymore, I said, "You mean like we don't for the Jehovah Witness," she laughed, which was the first time I had seen her smile since before Papa passed, she responded, "Exactly." One evening after this new rule was in place Aunt Rita stopped by the house and was met with some strong resistance from Grandma. Gloria's manipulative ways had caused

Grandma to treat her second eldest daughter like a leech, like a wandering vagabond, "Rita you can't be coming over here if you on that mess," Grandma said. "Momma let me in this house," Aunt Rita responded. She began pulling on the medal of the screen door rather irately and pulled a piece of it off. Grandma never let anyone in the house, so it took me a minute to realize it was my beloved Auntie that she was arguing with. I ran over to give Aunt Rita a hug which allowed her to slip inside the house. Grandma snuck off to call Gloria while I embraced Aunt Rita, it had been months since I last saw her, and I remember the hug like it was yesterday. About twenty minutes later I heard Gloria's deteriorating Nissan Sentra turn the corner from down the block, it always sounded like an overworked lawn mower that was shutting down after cutting its last lawn for the day. Her car puttered to a stop right outside the house. Our fence was lopsided, so it always made an annoyingly loud noise when someone opened it, but this day I just heard the car door slam loudly, and the fence was swung open so fast that it didn't make a sound. Shortly after she stormed inside a huge argument erupted between the two. "What's this shit about Gloria, you got momma not letting me in the house," Aunt Rita said. "Momma tell her to get out, she's a fucking crackhead," Gloria responded. "Really momma you going to listen to Gloria, she ain't never did shit but take from you." I didn't know whether to cry, or just grab the popcorn, but suddenly my eyes became affixed on Grandma, I had never seen her in such a matrix. I saw a seismic force weighing on her shoulders, choosing a penultimate side between her two daughters, shortly after the death of her husband. Grandma attempted to remain docile and urged them both to calm down, "This ain't how family supposed to talk to one another," Grandma said. The argument continued to escalate, which was particularly concerning for Gloria, who stood no chance in a fist fight against her younger sister. In addition to being an engineering graduate, Aunt Rita was also a black belt martial artist, and was seconds away from reminding Gloria of that critical fact. Before things got physical, I saw Gloria nervously pick up the phone and call the police. Grandma tried to stop her from calling the cops, but it was too late, and this would be the last night I ever saw my Aunt Rita. Grandma and Gloria met the cops outside so they would not see the deplorable conditions inside the house. I still remember standing at the screen door, the blue lights flashing against the backdrop of this blurry scene. Aunt Rita was emphatically pleading her case to the officer, but her lack of composure didn't seem to rub him well. *"They got my 6-year-old nephew in there, he doesn't have any food, and he sleeping on the floor, they got him living trifling,"* Aunt Rita said with pure sincerity in her voice. The officer positioned his face in my direction, as if to say, is this true? Standing at the screen door in my pajamas, I wanted to nod my head and say yes, but I did not, I just stood there, frozen. It seemed as if he was looking at me for centuries, but it was only a brief second. He immediately returned his attention to the ensuing chaos. The officer asked, "May I go inside?" "My son is tired I really rather we handle this outside," Gloria responded. Grandma and Gloria hadn't yet perfected their masterful art of concocting excuses for why would-be guests were not allowed inside the house, and I could tell the officer wasn't in love with her answer. But they did successfully paint the picture to the officer that Aunt Rita was a crackhead, and no longer welcome at the residence. Aunt Rita was pretty irate by the time I saw the police lights flashing outside the screen door, and she did very little to convince the officers otherwise. The police didn't bother to investigate her claim about my living conditions, and I was always regretful that they didn't. I didn't want to be there, especially if Aunt Rita would no longer be coming to visit. Aunt Rita forever holds a special place in my heart. A woman more concerned about my living condition than the woman who birthed me. A woman struggling with her own demons but exercised the wherewithal to advocate on my behalf. Every single night for seventeen years I prayed to God for a bed to sleep in, and not to have roaches and mice. My childhood prayers seemed to fall upon deaf ears, because year after year I remained right there, sleeping on the floor. I know dogs that were raised in better conditions than I was. Dogs whose owners dressed them in sleek outfits, ensure regular veterinary check-ups, have framed family pictures hanging on the walls, and are fed multiple times a day. I was not privy to a family vacation, framed family pictures, or even a decent home cooked meal. I never sat down at a dinner table for supper, folded clothes and placed them in a dresser, or hung posters in a bedroom. It was as if I existed only on paper, as nine numbers that allowed Gloria to secure a couple hundred dollars a month from my dad, but not in principal.

"When you are going through the process it can be difficult at times to see how all these lines connect or why some periods of silence or suffering are necessary"

Howard Falco - Time in a Bottle

Dear Momma

"Until the lion learns to write, every story will glorify the hunter"
Old African Proverb

Gloria was not your prototypical independent black mother from the 90's era. She had no burning motivation to prove her resilience and showcase her ability to provide for her only son alone. She did not relish in the satisfaction of putting food on the table, clothes on my back, and a roof over our head. If you searched the portfolios of every Dayton photographer from the 90's, you would find no mother-son pictures of us. Following my parents abrupt divorce, Gloria became even more emotionally confused, reluctantly swallowing the bitter cocktail of divorce and single motherhood. She remained haunted by her decision to invest the remainder of her roaring twenties on my dad, a man who calendared his evenings for smoking ganja, and spacing out to Bob Marley classics. I was an 8lb dumbbell that she refused to carry into her future. I was a crying, needy, and hungry reminder of a second failed marriage, a living, breathing barrier on the road to finding her next true love. She would not allow her maternal mistake to linger for the next eighteen years, but rather than leave me to the vices of the world, where a loving family might have taken me in, she sought out to systematically destroy me. She could have done a selfless act and given me to a family that would have given me a shot at a better life. A family with a house where I would have had my own room, a finished basement where I could invite friends over, and a kitchen where I could walk about without fear. But instead she created a sophisticated system of oppression that is the basis of my first seventeen years of life. A system I define as oppressive poverty. If her life was a resume, my birth was a small gap in employment, that awkward explanation during the job interview where you say that you decided to pursue other opportunities, my birth was the aha moment that inspired her to change career paths. So, she did, leaving my growth in the hands of her aging mother, a failing school district, and a dying community, but not before setting up the deadly parameters to ensure my destruction (like the rules to a rigged Hunger Games match). Gloria is a master manipulator and could

15

paint a vivid picture to outsiders that she was just your normal hard-working American mother. When relatives inquired about the condition of Grandma's home, she would often reply, "It's messy because momma never throws anything away." She planted delusions of grandeur in my head for nearly two decades. Every year my Grannie Payne on my dad's side purchased me a $100 U.S savings bond for Christmas, as my legal guardian she felt the need to "hold onto them for me," but I never saw them again. I innately knew that Gloria didn't do the hugging and kissing thing, but I remember us sharing a few moments prior to me turning four or five. I remember she took me to her job at DESC (Defense Electronics Supply Center) when I was three and taking me to Arthur O. Fisher Park to play on the jungle gym once. But these handful of instances were the exception, not the rule, and even they came to a screeching end when things between her and Derrick really took off. Grandma Clark was the closest thing I had to a mother; her name is tattooed on my left arm right above a sketch of my Grandpa Payne's face. Her name is not forever tattooed on me because she provided the nurturing one would expect from a mother, but because she was the soldier that I went to war with. I remember watching Grandma step over piles of trash as she walked to the refrigerator and feeling powerless as I watched her shoulders drop in disappointment upon remembering that we didn't have anything inside of it. After repeatedly bearing witness to cockroaches' crawl inside pots and pans I stopped eating the little food that was present in our humble excuse for a kitchen, but Grandma didn't mind the roaches and rats like I did.

For much of my childhood, my Uncle Art was a little on the heavier side, and I would often lobby for him to bring us some McDonald's on the days when he stopped by, which he usually did. Grandma would often whip herself up some oatmeal or Jiffy cornbread to suffice her hunger. Watching her sit on the floor or edge of our crumbling coach always reminded me of a slave being tossed mush down to the bottom of a slave hold. I was a young boy putting on his best Johnny Cochran impersonation, trying to present the facts of our situation to Gloria, in hopes of convincing her to throw away her unworn clothes, cheap jewelry, nostalgic high school memorabilia, and "important" papers from the 1970's, so her son and mother could have a bed to lay in.

"Mom you don't even wear this stuff, it's on the floor," I would sigh. Gloria was playing a high-level game of mental warfare, she systematically disconnected me from friends, other relatives, and my neighborhood. The conditions in the home were deplorable, the stench from overflowing garbage, intense heat, and hoarding was reprehensible, and my childhood demeanor was inseparable from my home conditions. Her hoarding is the centerpiece of our broken relationship. I've always been fascinated by our emptiness, for too many decades I've experienced that awkward moment where someone assumes I have a relationship with my mom, "I'm sure your mom spoiled you, look at them eyelashes," I always wanted to respond, "Actually no ma'am she didn't," or "I have not spoken to that lady in years," but instead I usually smile and wait for that awkward point in the conversation to shift. I refuse to get on social media or attend church on Mother's Day, the excessive outpouring of love and affection for obviously one of the most important relationships on the planet speaks to that gaping absence in my life. Her hoarding and treatment of Grandma and I caused the most innate bond, the one between a mother and her child, to become adversarial. After Gloria allowed me to hitch a ride to Earth, she wiped her hands of me, but not entirely, she maintained the financial incentives of my existence through social security scams and the State of Ohio child support system. When I finally escaped her clutches and found myself on a college campus, she used my social security number to illegally obtain credit cards and ran up astronomical bills in my name. In 2009 my wages were garnished while working as a host at Cracker Barrel due to a credit card she obtained in my name without my consent or knowledge. So, when people ask me why I don't talk to my mother the answer is simple, I never had one.

She tried to bury me but didn't know that I was a seed. A cyclone, a descendant of the great survivors. She had no idea that her attempts to destroy me would ultimately enhance my laser focus, and that I would develop all the parts of myself that she tried to destroy. She tried to cut me off from the light of Heaven but failed to realize that I am inseparable from the Creator, and that angelic light burns deep within me. She had no idea that I was unbreakable

ShoMari Payne - Chosen One

CHAPTER III
Come to Consciousness

In 1992 I was five years old, during this time I only fully knew the interior layout of two homes, Grandma Clark's home in West Dayton (Jefferson Township), and Grandpa and Grannie Payne's house in the suburbs of north Dayton (Vandalia, Ohio). Other homes I visited such as my Uncle Art's and Aunt Rita's had not provided me with a sufficient sample size to draw any real conclusions about my living conditions. But as time waned, I began visiting more friends' houses, and slept over at other relatives' homes. These experiences added crucial pieces of data to the growing curiosity I held towards my living conditions. Each new living room tour and bathroom visit was a piece of evidence towards my expanding logic. I was becoming conscious of my peculiar living standards and begun to piece together the clues to pinpoint my oppressor. I took detailed mental notes of the interior conditions of neighbors' homes, scanning the premise for signs of mice, mice traps, roaches, cans of Raid, and unkempt bathrooms. But collectively I never found anything that resembled my Grandmother's home. I generally found bunk beds, healthy refrigerators, clean garages that stored tools and bicycles, play areas, and small wooden desks for after school study. Was it Grandma who was responsible for the messy house I would ponder? She was a semi-hoarder in her own right, she would take notes incessantly of anything she heard, read, or saw on television. She would write in spiral notebooks and archive her writings on the fridge, or in piles on the living room floor. "Grandma you are never going to read this again, why do you save all this stuff," I would ask. She would pretend not to hear me and continue writing. Grandma would use old cans as pencil holders or to store loose change, she would collect the Dayton Daily Newspaper as some strange badge of honor and refused to throw away a paper. The dustiness in the house left Grandma with a wicked cough, and she always kept a roll of toilet paper near her so that she could spit out her phlegm, and then toss the tissue it into a plastic bag next to her on the floor. This was always hard for me to watch so I turned my head whenever she started coughing. Although Grandma found quirky ways to use household items, which I truly despised, she just didn't own enough items to submerge the house into that degree of clutter. She would use can goods, jars, and old paper platers to file away things of "value", but she also only owned two or three outfits, and the bedrooms were overflowing with clothes. By the age of six I concluded that Grandma was not the culprit, only a docile accomplice at best. I'm sure that Grandma's hoarding tendencies have roots in her humble beginnings in the South, from her intimate experience growing up only one generation after Emancipation. She literally came to Ohio with nothing, and psychologically feared letting go of the few items she had accumulated.

"Hoarding disorder is unique from other disorder because its symptoms are tangible and entail a large accumulation of objects that prevent the use of space necessary for usual human functions"
Randy Frost – Hoarding Expert

My bathroom at Grandma's

"Clutter creates obstacles that become health or safety hazards, slow the ability of first responders to act in emergencies, or simply impedes daily life activities"
Metropolitan Boston Housing Partnership

Papa was a rolling stone

"Boo-hoo, sad story, black American dad story"
Drake - Look What You've Done

As a boy, the days spent with my dad were some of the happiest of my childhood. For the first few years of my life, he was equally my hero as his father, my Grandpa Payne. My father was extremely pro-black, the kind of anti-establishment black man you'd find selling Muslim newspapers and bean pies in most inner-city intersections during the 90's or rocking a dashiki with the matching kufi at your local mall. He sees symbolism of government conspiracies and the plot to oppress the black race in every single movie, including Finding Nemo and the Lion King. He is supra talented, a retired graphic artist for the Federal Government, having designed artwork for military bases across the country. He is also a master guitarist, playing at a high level since the age of fourteen. Today you can find him jamming out in the top corner of his house, or in a small nightclub just a few miles east of downtown Columbus, Ohio. Our relationship has ebbed and flowed throughout my life. My earliest memories of Dad begin in the early 90's, when Grandma Clark or Gloria would coordinate my transfer to his apartment for the weekend. I don't remember who told me that he was my dad, or why I believed it, but after a few visits with him I accepted it as fact. I recall anxiously standing on Grandma Clark's front porch for his arrival. In those days he was driving a red Chevrolet Astro van, and he still had a nice afro on top of his head. Some days he would call to cancel, while I had already been standing on the porch for hours, and I would immediately hear the frustration in Grandma's voice while he attempted to explain his absence, "Okay Curtis, that boy show is going to be disappointed." But on the days, he did show up, I would sprint to his red Chevy Astro van and never look back.

"I was ready, fuck that I been ready, since my dad used to tell me he
was coming to the house to get me. He ain't show up.
Valuable lesson man I had to grow up"
Drake - 0 to 100

Dad was never once was allowed inside my Grandma's house, back then I wondered why he never questioned that peculiar regulation. A part of me wanted him to ask me questions about my home life, I'm sure I would have lied about the conditions, or used an excuse given to me prior by Gloria or Grandma. But maybe I would have told him what my Aunt Rita told the Dayton Police, that I was sleeping on the floor and living trifling. Maybe I would have told him that I didn't have a bedroom, and that I was probably the source of the few roaches in his apartment. And maybe he would have done something about it? That's what I like to tell myself anyway, but I have come to realize that people have selective vision and hearing, especially when it requires action on their behalf. In so many ways I did tell him, I told him through the plastic grocery bags of clothes and toiletries that served as the luggage I carried over to his low-income apartments. I told him through the stains and holes on my clothes, and the absence of manners and etiquette that would be expected for a child my age. Through simple things like not knowing how to properly hold a fork or knife, not knowing how to fold clothes, make a bed, or wash a dish. I told him through my grumbling stomach on our fifteen-minute ride to his apartment or to Grandpa and Grannie Payne's house, and through my cognitive dissonance towards anything associated with Gloria or Grandma Clark.

In 1996 Dad informed me that he was moving to Columbus, Ohio due to the closure of the DESC base in Kettering, Ohio. At the same time Gloria (who had already become a microscopic figure in my hierarchy of importance), acknowledged that she would now be working in Columbus as well due to the base closure. I wasn't sure why they both were leaving Dayton, after all that's where I was. I figured eventually they would have to find a new school for me in Columbus so that I could be near them. But neither of them made mention of space for my existence in this new economic equation, I was factored out and remained in the sole custody of Grandma Clark. I was a third grader, and I remember feeling abandoned by them both. The weekly check-ins from Gloria became as rare as my fathers promised bi-weekly visits back to Dayton. Before Dad moved to Columbus in 96, we would hang out at least once a month, adding up to roughly 12 times a year give or take. Dad would pick me up from my oppressive environment in whatever vehicle he was financing at the moment and carry me into a day ½ of normality. We would go to the movies, the gym, or visit Grandpa and Grannie in Vandalia. Sometimes we would just stay at his apartment in Trotwood and rent a mix of video games and movies from the Blockbuster video store down the street in *Consumer Square* shopping center. His apartments were full of books on Ancient Egypt, government conspiracies, karate, and personal development. Dad has always been full of wisdom and knowledge surrounding the black struggle. He would often talk to me about heroes that I thought were just black radicals, not the black leaders I heard about in school like Dr. King and Medgar Evers, but leaders like Marcus Garvey, Malcolm X, and Angela Davis. Dad always dressed as if he was ready for the next black revolution, or downtown African festival, and his apartments always smelled like incense from the annual Dayton black cultural fest. If the gap between our last visit had exceeded the standard deviation in our normal visitation curve, you could bet that he had found a new girlfriend. The financial burden that I, and my three older siblings presented in Dad's budget forced him to acquire a part-time position working for the Dayton Daily Newspaper, as a delivery man. The Dayton Daily Newspaper was always special to me, because I consistently helped both Dad and Grandma Clark as their sidekicks with this occupation. Almost every weekend that we spent together I would wake up at 3:00am to help Dad deliver papers. "You coming with me ShoMari or you staying here," he would ask, "I'm coming Dad." Crust in my eyes, teeth unbrushed, I'd pop up off his black leather couch, layer up in clothes, and venture to the Dayton Daily News warehouse where we would put together what felt like an endless amount of newspapers. The Sunday paper was always a rather complex Rubik's cube to accurately solve. You had so many ads to stuff in the already thicker than normal paper, and sometimes we even had to fit a small box of cereal inside. Looking back, I guess it was like a sweatshop, and I was surely child labor. After putting together our inventory, we would stuff his van with several hundred papers, and venture into the thick morning fog for the next four hours. We drove up and down various neighborhoods, tossing papers onto front porches. We divided our workload into four sections, and by the time we reached section 4 the sun was at full steam, and I knew we were almost done with our days' work. Before we began our deliveries, Dad would grab himself a coffee from Speedway, and if he remembered he would grab me a sports drink. Upon the completion of our deliveries Dad would always let me keep a Sunday paper for myself, which made me so happy. I would fantasize about the day I could afford all the gadgets in the Best Buy and Circuit City ads, then I'd circle the items that I planned to buy first.

My synopsis of my dad was simple, a pro-black conspiracy theorist that was good at everything he touched artistically. He served a short stint in the U.S Army, and then began his career working for the Federal Government. But in 1996, the landscape of our relationship suffered a cosmic shift. Tension brewed in my heart for his decision to abandon me, and our crumbling city of Dayton that we together called home, for the glimmering economic opportunities that awaited in the States Capitol. I couldn't quite articulate it like that back then, but that was exactly how I felt. I don't think that I had ever been to Columbus, and never really had a desire to go. Everything I needed could be found in Dayton, just not at my Grandma's residence. My friends were in Dayton, my favorite cousins, and most importantly Grandpa & Grannie Payne. I still remember the smell of every apartment complex Dad stayed at, and I can name every vehicle he financed, the Chevrolet Astro van, a silver Chrysler van, a white Ford Taurus, a dark grey Mercury Mountaineer, and a dark blue Chevrolet Trailblazer. I remember these cars, because I recall the joyous feeling and deep disappointment of waiting for each of those makes and models to turn onto my Grandmas street. Many weekends the high demands of being a lady's man would place me on the back nine of his priorities at a moment's notice. Adding a 70-mile excuse to my dad's repertoire was a sort of death to the bond we had built over the previous nine years. All the weekends playing Sega Genesis at his apartments, watching movies that I was too young to watch like *He Got Game*, and waking up at the crack of dawn to help deliver newspapers are memories I will always cherish. But moments like these were now in the backdrop of our relationship, Columbus created a new normal for us, the relocation of his priorities.

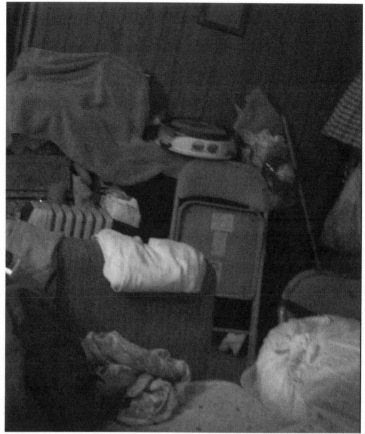

Grandma's bed

CHAPTER IV
Blairwood Elementary

In the first grade I was given a label, "gifted." This label required me to complete additional, more advanced school work, but I found tremendous pride in this recognition. A handful of my "gifted" classmates and I would tackle accelerated material and we carried higher academic expectations than our peers. One of those classmates in the gifted cohort was my dear friend Anthony Marsh aka Tony.

Majority of my earliest grade school memories include Tony. I remember in the 1st grade we were given a more challenging set of words for our spelling assignments, words like "Mississippi" and "Cincinnati." In the second grade I remember him edging me out for the role of Aladdin in the school play, which caught him the attention of my childhood crush (I was only a little bitter). Blairwood Elementary served students from Kindergarten to 4th grade, of which I attended 1st through 4th. The gifted portion of our experience culminated at the end of the third grade, but that year our gifted section was combined with about five 4th grade students who were also given a label, "troubled" and "at-risk." This was also the year that I ran into my first pair of real bullies, Eric Raglin and Jaron Lewis (funny how we never forget the government name of our first bullies). They were 4th graders who would be spending a large portion of the academic year with us. Half of our day was spent in the gifted section, in which our 4th grade companions were not with us, during this time we studied math, reading, and science. During the second half of the day we shared the learning environment, during this time we studied our less rigorous subjects such as social studies, Physical Education, health, and recess. Ironically, it was in the third grade when I felt the decline of my academic advantage. I remember mastering my multiplication tables before the rest of my peers as a second grader but struggling mightily when introduced to division and fractions. Most of all, I vividly remember struggling to physically see the chalkboard, due to my astigmatism and very poor vision. One day in second grade I recall sitting in class while my teacher Ms. Gulf was explaining fractions, I went to reach into my backpack for a pencil and my eyes became affixed on a gigantic cockroach that I saw crawling out of it. My first inclination was to stand up and draw attention to the bug, yelling something out, "Aw hell nah this school dirty as fuck," but I figured it'd be best to keep this between me and the roach, we both know where he resided.

My first physical encounter with Eric and Jaron occurred in the third grade on the playground. We were playing kickball at recess and Jaron had cut me several times. After the fourth cut I decided it was high time I grew a pair, or this would set the stage for an entire year of being punked. "Hey man it's my turn," as I eased in front of him, "Move bitch," he responded emphatically, which prompted a large ooooooo among all the playground kids. Embarrassed by this verbal punking, I responded with a trusty rebuttal, "Your momma." Jaron proceeded to wail on me, and his buddy Eric jumped in for a piece of the action. I was much smaller than them both, and I never understood why Eric felt the need to jump in, Jaron had me under control by himself. After a few good minutes of stomping, my good friend Leshea intervened and exclaimed, "That is enough!" Leshea was tall, athletic, and in our eyes the next Lisa Leslie, she commanded the respect of the entire school. I had the biggest crush on Leshea that year, and I'm pretty sure her saving me from an ass whooping did me no favors in that department. Eventually an administrator dispersed the crowd and marched all three of us to the office. I remember Eric and Jaron laughing and pointing to my right eye that was pulsating profusely, as we walked to the Principal's office. I explained my minimal role in the altercation to the Principal, and they indeed became my enemies for the entire school year.

Kimmel Lane

"I used to hit the kitchen lights, cockroaches everywhere"

Young Jeezy - Thug Motivation 101

Grandma's house was always dark, gloomy, and very depressing. Gloria would tell Grandma and I to never open our stained brown curtains too far, so that no one passing by was able to see the chaos inside the house. This regulation allowed for little light to enter the living room, the section where Grandma and I spent 99% of our time. The darkness of the living room always struck me as an intentional method to break my spirit. The second I stepped inside the house upon arriving from school I was no longer able to fake my happiness. I would enter the house and immediately see Grandma sitting on the couch, eating cornbread from a napkin, watching her stories on a small television, I would see roaches crawling on the wall, and the smell immediately engulfed me, "Hurry up

27

and shut the door ShoMari, don't want people looking all in the house," Grandma would say in a hurried voice. The darkness of the living room reminds me of a quote I read referring to a time right before the eve of the Civil War, when the overwhelming majority of the slave population was illiterate, a situation that most Southern whites favored. A delegate to the Virginia House of delegate boasted about how the process of slavery was working masterfully during a meeting.

"We have as far as possible closed every avenue by which light may enter their minds. If we could extinguish the capacity to see the light our work would be completed."

Papa's old room

Grandma's living room

"Behavior is key; it's really a problem with behavior. Clearing things out isn't going to solve that. The clutter will come back unless something is done to change the person's behavior"
Randy Frost – Hoarding Expert

Gloria made frequent proclamations to "straighten up the house," on the weekends, but the weekends came and went, and she never changed the circumstances for us. On the rare occasion she made good on her word, she would stop by for a few hours, slide on her disinfectant gloves and mask, then literally climb over piles of junk and begin her "sorting" process. Even as a child I found it highly ironic that we were forced to live amiss the hoarding, the unsafe, inhumane conditions of her doing, but we were provided no such protective gear for our daily toil. We inhaled the sewer-like smells from our frequently out of order bathroom, ate processed meals on paper plates, and watched cockroaches crawl up and down the microwave and into our Hungry Man TV dinners. We could not light a candle, because one mishap and the house would go up in flames. We had no sanitation for our hands and slept on floors soiled by rodents. I remember seeing rat droppings all over the house, in my clothes, and throughout the kitchen, which was always disheartening. Finding chew marks from rats on my clothes and being forced to wear them to school, made me feel violated in a way that I know my peers would never understand. But there she was, dressed like a professional bug exterminator, navigating through her own land field. She would store items in totes with no sense of organization or distinguishable system. She would move masses of unworn clothes from one room, and shift her high school memorabilia, pictures, sewing machines, old jewelry, VHS tapes, wired hangers, and newspaper clippings to the other. It was all a charade to convince us that she was invested in making the house a livable environment. A part of her problem was that she really wasn't that poor, only Grandma and I lived below the poverty line, and her steady income as a Government employee allowed for a continual circulation of new clothes on top of the fact, she never threw anything away. Gloria had filed several bankruptcies and used retail shopping stores as an ATM in times of a financial crunch. I remember accompanying her to Marshall's, Value City, and Burlington Coat Factory and watching her pull out hundreds of receipts and conduct what appeared to be stock trading with the poor associate. "No, you're not listening, I said cancel this layaway, and move the leather jacket to this layaway (hands associate a different receipt), then I want to put the pants on a new layaway, and you owe me back $20 sweetheart." As I grew older, I began strengthening my arguments for the removal of her hazardous trash from the house, hoping my articulation would light a fire of action. I started mentioning agencies such as Child Protective Services, the Dayton Police, and the zoning department. "You can go to jail for this," I would exclaim. "This place is a fire hazard," I'd yell, but she wasn't the least bit worried. "ShoMari who is going to believe you, look at your report card, and your teachers keep calling the house," she would say in a dismissive voice. My deviant behavior at school and declining grades were here go to rebuttal, and deep down she knew that I feared the potential ridicule of my peers and would not risk opening that can of worms. I remember two kids in my district were locked in the basement by their parents, when the story came out it was the talk of the town, I never wanted that kind of publicity, but I felt a deep connection to their oppression. I contemplated setting the house on fire and watching all of her possessions turn into smoke, the only problem was Grandma was always home, and I wasn't trying to harm Grandma or get caught, I just wanted to see the look on Gloria's face when she pulled up to the house and all of her shit was destroyed.

I remember the exterminator came once, and he was visibly repulsed by the decrepit conditions, he made it clear upon his initial walkthrough, "You guys have way too much stuff in here, I can't guarantee anything, too many places for them to hide and breed." His words cut right through the high expectations that I held. I was so hopeful that he would get rid of the roaches, and then the rats. For about a week after his fumigation visit, I noticed a small decline in the roaches crawling across the walls, and even wondered if I could walk into the kitchen without my shoes on. But the next week they were back, strong as ever, inside of our old wooden cabinets, crawling up and down our outdated oven, and into the rusted steel pot of boiling water that Grandma used to cook our oatmeal.

I'll always remember this day; I was around 7 years old helping Grandma with some yard work. Frustrated with picking dandelions I posed Grandma with the question, "Why we worried about the outside of the house, but the inside is fucked up?" Grandma chased after me for cursing and I stopped on the side of the house and picked up a brick. "ShoMari you better put that brick down," Grandma said in an unsure voice. I was never going to hit her, but I hadn't thought far enough ahead on what I was going to do next, so I launched it towards a window of the house out of frustration. I surely hadn't accounted for the fact that Uncle Art was stopping by that day, and that he would hand me one of the worse whooping's I ever had. Lastly, I never thought that the

31

window would never get fixed, and that we would just put a black trash bag over it for the next decade. The cold air that rushed in through the broken window during the winter months was unbearable. The entire house was an icebox every fall night and all winter, and as I grew older, I always regretted that I was the one responsible for the broken window. We had received several warnings from city regarding the condition of our crumbling garage door and collapsing gutters that the house would be inspected or fined if action wasn't taken. I figured that the conditions outside the house should have been a huge red flag for a city agency to investigate deeper, because there was a lot more going on than sinking gutters. Due to this citation, Gloria and Grandma hired someone to repair the garage, but no such services were provided for the interior of the home. Outside of the house you would usually find 2-5 non-operational junk cars, all with flat tires. The cars belonged to a combination between my Uncle Art, Gloria, and Aunt Nancy. There was a rusty silver 92 Nissan, a rusty red 77 Malibu, a 2-door two tone yellow and red 92 Ford Escort, a 96 rusting Pontiac Grand Am with a cracked windshield, and a red 88 Chevy Cavalier with tinted windows. These all made for a huge laugh when the school bus would pass by my house. I could hear several students making snarky remarks every time I entered or exited the school bus, "Who live der," or "Bruh that's a piece of shit," I pretended not to hear them, and would usually keep walking past Grandma's house after getting off the bus, pretending that wasn't my home, hoping as few students as possible knew that I was the kid living there. This proved not to be a sustainable strategy, eventually everyone found out that I indeed was the kid living in the most physically unattractive house in the district. So, I adopted a new strategy, operation get off the bus at a friend's house. By the time I became a teenager I was deeply invested in protecting the family secret. Revealing the truth about my living conditions might ostracize me even further from friends and family. I feared that the handful of friends that were willing to accept me inside their homes might shut their doors if they knew the truth.

Grandma's house

"The fridge so empty it's hurting yo self-esteem"
Meek Mill

"Can I spend the night"

As a child, the recurring question that I posed to my peers on a weekly basis was, "Can I spend the night?" When the parents of my childhood friends saw *937-262-8640* flash across their caller ID, I'm sure their hearts sank to their stomach. It was a guarantee that I either wanted to come over to eat or spend the night. I can't blame them, the one-sidedness of being my friend was not a value-add for the parents in my neighborhood. "Why can't people ever come over your house ShoMari," some parents would ask while I was eating at their dinner tables. These mounting inquisitions forced me to develop a system of rotating weekends so that my presence did not become too cumbersome on any particular family member or set of friends. First on my list was always Uncle Art, he lived on the westside of the city with his girlfriend and her son Chris. I loved going over their house and hanging out with my talented and cultured older cousin. Chris taught me how to hoop, indoctrinated me into No Limit & Cash Money rap records, and allowed me to clip out pictures from his Source and Slam magazines. We would create our own makeshift photo albums and hood vision boards, "Nah nigga you can't get the Foxy Brown, she mine," he once told me with a serious mug painted across his face. I still remember lusting over the voluptuous image of the rapper "Foxy Brown" laced in purple lingerie. Chris interrupted my daydream, reminded me again that she was his woman, and snatched the magazine out of my disappointed hands. Chris would take me to all the hood parks in the city, and to open gyms at McFarland, Bomberger, Princeton, and Roosevelt to play ball. I sucked pretty bad back then, but Chris would still allow me to tag along, and get in some crucial reps. Chris had some of the best handles in the city, and he openly shared his secrets of ball handling with me. We would stay in the house all day studying AND1 Mixtapes, rewinding certain moves, and then go outside to ingrain our new skills. If Chris and I weren't hooping, we would walk up and down West Third street just looking for shit to get into. We would walk to Broaster hut, a chicken spot on West Third street to pick up large orders that his mom and Uncle Art had placed. We would walk to corner stores to get boxes of cereal, bologna, and gallons of Chilly Willy juice for the house, or post up at *HomeBoyz Music*, a local music store that was just down the street. Chris was a huge WCW & WWF fan, and we would have iconic wrestling matches in the basement. On rainy days we'd lock ourselves in the house, turn on DMX's *It's Dark & Hell is Hot* album, and play video games all day. Whether it was Street Fighter or Tomb Raider, all we needed was some music, bowls of cereal, and the video game, and we'd become zombies for days on in. I remember one winter my elementary school was closed for nearly two extra weeks beyond the Christmas break. Every morning I would turn on the news and pray that *Jefferson Township School District Closed* would arrive on the screen so I could tell Uncle Art that I could extend my sleepover. Chris was always fresh, and sometimes he would hand me down a pair of his old kicks so I wouldn't be so dusty. "Here my nigga you can borrow these Space Jam's, just don't fuck em up," as he handed me the only pair of Jordan's I ever wore, even though they weren't my size. Chris and I are cousins, even though we don't see each other much these days, he was someone who looked out for me back when not many people were.

Cousin in jail again, asking me for bail again
Close when I was 12, but I was much frailer then
He was like 16, a nigga from the gutter and
Years ago his favorite uncle had married my mother and
Here we are, runnin' through the Ville like dumb and dumber and
For that summer man I swear I wish you was my brother then
J. Cole – Cousins

Home Boyz Music - Dayton, Ohio

The next weekend visitation house on the list was my first Cousin Ali, who lived in Huber Heights, Ohio. Our dads are brothers, which allowed for plenty of obligatory opportunities for us to build a bond. I would coordinate weekends for us to meet up at our Grandparents house in Vandalia, or I would spend the weekend at his crib. Ali and his mom, my Aunt Cynthia, always made me feel welcome in their home, even though Ali had never stepped foot inside mine. I would go over Ali's house on Friday nights, get up Saturday mornings and sit in the stands to watch him participate in pee-wee football games in the Fall, and basketball tournaments in the Spring. They maintained a refrigerator full of food, and Aunt Cynthia was never was stingy with ordering us a Large pepperoni pizza. The one-sided trips to Ali's house added up rather quickly, and early on in our relationship Aunt Cynthia would inquire about this discrepancy, but eventually, she quit questioning this peculiar regulation.

Next was my Aunt Nancy, she stayed on the westside in Parkside Housing Projects, and moved to the Northland housing projects a few years later. She had a daughter, my cousin Whitney, whom was like my little sister. I felt responsible for Whitney and always vowed to have her back. I remember making bologna sandwiches for the both of us while Aunt Nancy would run errands or go to work. We would play on the playgrounds at Parkside and Northland for hours on end. Whitney and I built a hundred forts, shared many meals, and established a bond that will always remain. She was one of the few people who were aware of the conditions at Grandma Clark's house, but she was too young to understand that it wasn't normal.

Parkside housing projects - Dayton, Ohio

Last on the list were my childhood best friends Tony Marsh and Torrey Parker. Tony, lived in the same neighborhood that I did, but he resided in one of the nicest houses in the area. Lots of our childhood friends would pile over to Tony's house for a weekend slumber party in his basement. I remember one weekend in particular when my homeboys Deshawn, AC, and Corey all brought over our Walkman's and a combination of Cash Money & No Limit cd's and thugged it out all weekend in Tony's basement. Tony's parents always showed me love and understanding, allowing me to hitch a ride from school, to work, to driver's ed, or just inviting me inside for a home cooked meal. Torrey and I rode the same bus in middle school, and our friendship began in the 4th grade. I learned to intentionally start an intense conversation with Torrey right before his bus stop, then just follow him off the bus so we could continue. "Nigga why did you get off at my house," he would ask. But after this brief interrogation he'd invite me in, and we would hang out for hours. Both Tony and Torrey were always welcoming, and understanding, even though I never shared with them the secret about my house, and like everyone else, they were never permitted to enter.

Children of hoarding family members who lived in moderate or greater clutter before age 10 reported significantly more distress than did those who lived in less clutter prior to age 10: they rated their childhoods as less happy, reported more difficulty making friends, had people over less often, argued with parents more, described their relationship with their parents as more strained, and were more embarrassed about the condition of the home.

International OCD Foundation

CHAPTER V
Vandalia, Ohio

As bad as I had it on the westside of Dayton at Grandma's house, I held onto the fact that most weekends I could escape to what I felt was a mansion, a 3 bedroom, 2.5 bath ranch nestled quietly in the suburbs, of Dayton in Vandalia, Ohio. Grandpa & Grannie Payne were the best thing to ever happened to me. They were truly a Godsend from the heavens above. It was at their home and under their tutelage that I finally learned how to do division, cut grass, shovel snow, properly use a fork and knife, wash clothes, solve puzzles, play monopoly, watch cable television, and eat fluffy buttermilk pancakes. Grandpa had a certain jenesequa that seemed to radiate throughout the entire neighborhood, really the entire community. Everything that Grandpa did, he brought a disciplined precision to the task. Oftentimes Grannie Payne would become frustrated with the interior design of her kitchen, and Grandpa would head to ACE hardware, purchase an assortment of wood and all the tools necessary to undertake a remodeling venture. He built a woodshed in the backyard, cut down trees, mowed the grass, planted gardens, built beautiful wood-finished cabinets from scratch, and added an entire deck connecting their upstairs bedroom to the backyard. Grandpa and I went on thousands of adventures and he taught me a million lessons. He was a minister at Zion Baptist Church, and all of the church members revered Grandpa for his seemingly infinite wisdom, genuine spirit, and giving heart.

Grandpa & Grannie Payne's house - Vandalia, Ohio

They had one of those old school big screen TV's in the living room, a grand piano which Grannie Payne played eloquently, and a backyard full of trees and land where my siblings and Cousin Ali would learn all the life lessons necessary to overcome anything we could imagine. Grandpa cooked us all a five-star breakfast every Saturday morning that we spent the night, and Grandma prepared a scrumptious dinner every Sunday afternoon following church. They gave us money when we were in a crunch, purchased us U.S savings bonds, and had a floor full of gifts ready for us all every Christmas morning. This was the place where I learned normality, and I will never discount the profound impact they had on my life. Unfortunately, many kids who grow up like me do not have an angel like Grandpa Payne. I don't know what he saw in me during that stage of my life, but his love continues to manifest through me to this very day. Grandpa and Grannie were not wealthy, but they lived comfortably, like you would expect two hard-working sixty-year old's to live in the 90's. I did not sleep on the floor at their home, and there were no roaches except the ones I would bring with me, but Grandpa Payne would kill them and never utter a word to Grannie Payne about them.

In addition to my dad, they also had another son, Barry. Uncle Barry was Dad's younger brother, and the father to my cousin Ali. Uncle Barry lived in D.C during my childhood and worked as an Air Traffic Controller. Ali was only two years younger than me, so we grew up doing everything together, we were a package deal. Uncle Barry would fly into Dayton every summer and stay for several weeks at Grandpa and Grannie Payne's home. Ali would head over to our Grandparents house, and I would abruptly follow. Although Uncle Barry was primarily coming to Dayton to visit his son and his parents, he soon figured out that he'd be footing restaurant tabs for his humble nephew as well. Uncle Barry was a Godsend, exposing me to places like Dave & Busters, sports bar restaurants, Kings Island Amusement Park, Cincinnati Bengals games, Cincinnati Reds games, Cap'n Bogeys, laser tag, Vandalia Rec Center, and the Newport Aquarium. In the beginning of our excursions he would ask, "Did your mom send any money over with you," but eventually he stopped asking, which made me feel accepted in his eyes. If it wasn't for Uncle Barry I would have very few childhood highlights, but thanks to him when I returned to school every fall, I always had a story or two to share. These experiences helped provide a necessary boost to my diminishing confidence. Uncle Barry ultimately relocated to Ohio to better support Ali during his high school years.

Back to Reality

As awesome as my weekends were when I was able to escape, the lion's share of my childhood was spent at Grandma Clark's house. I recall one night during childhood when the drive of hunger masked my usual fear of entering our desolate kitchen after the sun had fallen, and I entered in hopes of overlooking a tasty snack during my earlier quest. There were many unwritten rules that I adopted to survive in that house and entering the kitchen after sun fall was near the top of my list. But this night I was particularly starving, so I patiently listened for the usual late-night agility sessions of the mice, and after a few minutes of silence I was delighted that they probably moved their training to another part of the house for the evening. I made my way to the kitchen and as I opened the refrigerator door four gigantic mice sprinted from the bottom of the fridge. I remember screaming to the top of my lungs as they rushed out dispersing throughout the house. I ran to the living room and jumped on top of the couch, awaking Grandma. "Grandma wake up, I just saw four rats in the refrigerator, can you go in there," I was hoping her fearless southern spirit would bring some peace to my unrest. She grudgingly arose and searched the kitchen only to find nothing. I insisted that I slept beside her on our decrepit couch, sacrificing her physical comfort, for my emotional. This experience had done it for me, I was emotionally broken, and I didn't open the refrigerator door or step inside the kitchen for weeks. This happened more nights than I can count. I would call Gloria at her boyfriend Derrick's house on these nights, but she never answered. On the rare nights I was able to get ahold of her, she would unenthusiastically say, "Tell momma to put some traps down," and abruptly hang up. Although I was young, I was not dumb, I knew the level of infestation we had couldn't be solved by putting some traps down or cans of raid, I wanted a permanent fix. Why couldn't my house look like Derrick's, and why don't you take your shit over there where you actually live, I would think to myself. I had been over Derricks house a couple of times, it was your typical clean house, there were beds, a healthy refrigerator, cupboards full of snacks, a big screen TV, no roaches in the kitchen, and his two sons even called Gloria mom. Around this time, I began to research the condition of hoarding, and point out the findings to Gloria and Grandma. "I'm not no damn hoarder," Gloria said to me in a combative voice. I started wondering if she could help her condition, and almost began to feel an ounce of sympathy. Is this mental or intentional, I would ponder, but I concluded the latter. I found no sympathy for a woman who would subject her son and mother to such adverse conditions while sleeping peacefully in a king sized bed, with leopard printed sheets, across town in a home fully furnished, walkable, sanitized, and equipped to support a normal state of existence. The handful of visits to Derricks confirmed the chaos at Kinmel Lane was by design. Gloria lived a completely different life at Derrick's off Philadelphia Avenue, night and day from the one Grandma and I were subjected to. You mean she is capable of cleaning, not having her shit everywhere, I thought to myself. She knew there was something psychologically crippling about rodents and cockroaches in the place you are forced to call home. These creatures seem to only congregate in places of failure. They have a way of reminding you daily that you are at the bottom of society. In the media these figures tend to only be found in dumpsters, abandoned buildings, and films about life in the projects. But in my life these creatures dominated the place that I slept, ate, and prayed.

Grandma Clark's house

Another reason that I knew our situation was beyond the scope of normality was when Grandma's siblings from down South would make the eight-hour trek from Alabama to Ohio to visit us, but even they were not permitted to step inside the house. Grandma and I would greet them outside and enjoyed our salutations from the pavement. They were not permitted to step inside no matter the temperature, they couldn't even come in to use our bathroom after their long journey, these are folks in their twilight years, yet we would point them in the direction of the closest McDonald's to use the restroom. This newfound treatment that Grandma directed towards her siblings began to drive a wedge between them, and they all became very puzzled. "Alice we've always been welcome in your house, what's going on," my great Uncle John once asked while standing in our front yard. I remember once my cousin Tiffany insisted that she had to use the restroom really bad, her Grandma, my Aunt Esther, said to my Grandma, "Alice my God will you let this girl come in and use the restroom." I was praying Grandma stuck by her guns and didn't fold to her younger sister's demand, I was so embarrassed that my cousin Tiffany would see how I was living. But Grandma and Gloria were semi-prepared for a hiccup, and conveniently covered up the junk in the living room with towels, sheets, and blankets to try and mask the hoarding. "We trying to get the place together, y'all excuse the mess," Grandma said while walking Tiffany past the scattered clothes, overflowing rubber maids, piles of newspapers, and bags trash. Grandma sat right outside the door while Tiffany used the bathroom, she didn't want her looking inside any of the bedrooms upon her exit. But more often than not Grandma presented our family members with her go-to excuse, "Our bathroom ain't working right now." After they realized this new normal, moving forward we would receive a call saying that they weren't going to be stopping by on this particular trip, and continued onwards to Detroit to visit Aunt Esther. But when they did stop by, we confined their visit to the front yard. Gloria would miraculously disappear and was completely inaccessible by phone when her Aunt's, Uncle's, and cousins would stop by to visit, she knew they would interrogate, pry, and ultimately force her to address the madness, and living conditions that Grandma was subjected to.

Front yard visit with Uncle C, Aunt Mildred, me, and Grandma

Teenage Years

Growing up I had a dog, his name was Dino, technically he was my Uncle Arts dog, but he remained in the custody of Grandma and I. Dino was a Pitbull mixed with American bulldog, he was white with spots and was blessed with a mean set of teeth. I was terrified of Dino for a year or so but eventually he began to show me infinite love. Being chained to a doghouse within a falling fence was a vulnerable location for a dog in my neighborhood, juvenile kids would throw rocks, or shoot BB guns at Dino frequently. Gloria refused to allow Dino to step one paw inside the house and risk potentially damaging any of her precious items. This wasn't so bad for majority of the months out of the year, but in the winters, he would be damn near freezing to death. I just knew one winter day I was going to go outside to call Dino and I wouldn't hear his chain drag across the pavement, that I would find him lifeless, frozen to death. Many days I would think to myself, what separates me from Dino, he's chained to a dilapidated excuse for a dog house, forced to remain outside in the freezing cold, never allowed inside the house, and I'm forced to stay in this freezing house, while Gloria lives a life of luxury. Uncle Art stuffed the dog house with hay to help keep Dino warm, but from watching him shake and barely cling to life, I'm doubtful of the hay's insulation capabilities against the relentlessness of an Ohio winter. During those treacherous winters I would bundle up, step outside, walk past several nonoperational cars, and go pet Dino, just to let him know that he wasn't completely forgotten. Dino and I had many conversations, and I still remember the way he looked at me when he would crawl out from his small wooden box. Dino would look at me with sad, tired eyes, and I knew he was furious that he couldn't come inside, even for a moment. I wanted to tell him, "Nigga it ain't that much better in there, trust me." Our heat was from frequently off, either due to nonpayment, or because the circuit breakers were weak. So, if Grandma and I had too many space heaters on at once, sometimes the power to the house would just cut off. I remember one winter we could see our breath inside the house, the Christmas tree was up, and Gloria was comfortably over Derricks and had called to wish us a Merry Christmas. I wanted to go over Grandpa Payne's for Christmas that day, but I remember watching Grandma cry after she hung up the phone, and I knew that I couldn't leave her there alone, with no heat. Dino lived a long life, and he eventually died ironically during the summer, I always thought the winter would take him out, but he was resilient, unfortunately life with us gave him no other choice.

The summer before seventh grade Grandpa Payne took me to the Base Exchange (BX) on Wright Patterson Air Force Base to purchase me a regulation basketball rim. Grandpa and I put the rim together in his driveway, and then hauled it to Grandma Clark's house so I would have some positive entertainment. I would drag the rim out from within our fence, onto the street, and shoot hoops for hours. Basketball became a true outlet for me during my childhood. Thanks to Grandpa's investment, in the seventh grade I made the basketball team at Radcliff Heights Middle school. Coach Mayfield wasn't too impressed by my atrocious tryout, but he told me that I had potential. That was an awesome year, even though I hardly garnered any playing time, it was a bonding experience for me. That year I kind of forgot that I was sleeping on the floor, and that I was rotating between the same two FUBU jerseys every day at school. I loved sports, but playing organized sports seemed like something that would be largely inaccessible for me moving forward. Sports seemed like a privilege for those who had at least one parent who valued their interests, not for kids like me. During basketball season I would get off the school bus at Torrey's house on days we had practice, hang out for several hours, hitch a ride with his mom to practice, and then pray she would be willing to take me home afterwards. Grandma Clark didn't drive, Dad lived in Columbus, and Gloria might as well have lived on another planet. Although I was comfortable catching public transportation, my school's rural location was not on the bus-line, which meant either I was hitching a ride home or walking a significant distance in the dark. A few nights I chose not to bum a ride from friends and walked the four-five miles home in the darkness. Moving forward my focus would be on making money and purchasing a car. I figured if sports were going to be part of my future, I'd have to pick them back up after I turned sixteen. Thankfully the State of Ohio allowed me to begin legal employment at the age of fourteen, which is when I landed my first full-time job during the summer 2001, as a janitor for my middle school.

"I know the feeling of being powerless to a system, the feeling of your future hanging in the balance, on trial, and your oppressor playing the role of judge and jury. An economic slave in the land of opportunity. I know the feeling of pleading for cosmic justice and counting down to a release date. I know what it is like to be a prisoner"
ShoMari Payne - Praying for my release

CHAPTER VI
Jefferson High School
(2001-2005)

I strategically missed between 60-70 days of high school each academic year between 2001-2005, collectively amounting to skipping over an entire year of high school. The first reason for skipping was that I feared my classmates ridicule, they made fun of my extreme acne breakouts, which were fueled by the stress from my adverse environmental conditions. My second reason for skipping was that I felt a daily anxiety sleeping on the floor with rats and cockroaches, and I feared bringing any roaches to school as I had done in times past. I hated wearing the same few shirts to school, as fashion held a colossal reverence in my high school, like most other urban black high schools in America. We were less concerned about who had the highest SAT scores, but deeply invested in who was wearing the latest Jordan's, and who wasn't. I on the other hand was not only without new shoes and clothes coming in, but washed my few shirts by hand, and then hung them in the backyard on a clothesline that Grandma had planted in the ground like a patriotic flag. I never had a dresser or closet, so I kept my school clothes next to me in a black trash bag, and on the days I did go to school, I would shake my outfit incessantly as my first line of defense against the roaches. I ate, slept, read, dreamed, grew, did sit-ups, and lived majority of my life on a small spot on the living room floor. That's where my pallet was, and that was my "room." As much as I hated that place, most days I figured it was better to stay at that filthy house, because I had learned to survive there.

"If everyone threw all their problems in a pile, majority of people would pick their own back up, they know how to deal with those problems"
Debbie Coleman - Professor - Miami University

This is a small list of the rules that I developed to adapt to the environment at Grandmas house. I remember writing them in a spiral notebook, along with poems and scriptures that I wrote down to uplift my spirit.

Rule #1. Do not to enter the kitchen if I heard any noise, that was the rodent's way of telling me to stay out.

Rule #2. After you survey the interior of the fridge for a few seconds, you only have about 5 more seconds to slam the door and sprint to the couch before a roach or rat scurried across your feet.

Rule #3. Never step in the kitchen without shoes/socks, rat droppings were always on the kitchen floor

Rule #4. Turn the empty microwave on high for three minutes before putting any food inside, this usually killed all the roaches that were in there.

Rule #5. Skip school if my acne was too bad, if my clothes were too smelly, or if I forgot to sit my backpack outside the night before.

Rule #6. Never let the pizza man come inside, even if it was 0 degrees outside and I was scrambling to add up change.

Rule #7. Fan and shake all your clothes thoroughly before putting them on, to try and get the roaches off.

Rule #8. Tie your trash bag tight or else the rats will rummage through your bag and you will have chew marks on your school clothes

Rule #9. You must meet anyone outside before they even have a chance to knock on the front door.

There were many other rules to survival that I adopted over the years, and by my senior year of high school I had mastered them all.

State of Ohio

"My future hinged more on passing my driver's license test than any grade I could have achieved in high school"
Buckeye Nights - ShoMari Payne

After my summer-long janitorial role ended, I knew that I needed to secure some other form of employment. There was no better feeling than having a few dollars in my pocket and exercising some power over my circumstances. I was no longer forced to digest the roach-infested cuisine at the house but could catch the bus up the street to McDonald's at a moment's notice. I could now offer gas money to friends, their parents, and other relatives for their sacrifices of picking me up and dropping me off. My second job was at McDonald's in Centerville, Ohio a predominately white, affluent suburb, that was a 20-25-minute drive from my house, but for me it was two-hour bus ride. I took two buses (sometimes three), the #22 from Grandmas to downtown Main & Third street, then once downtown a transfer to the X5, or I could get off the #22 on Germantown & Gettysburg, then catch the #24 southbound towards the Dayton Mall, which required an additional 2-mile walk. I kept this job for several months, mainly because of the 50% discount on employee meals. Tony and I worked our first two jobs together, but our conflicting work schedules made it difficult to always catch a ride with him out to McDonald's. I knew that getting my Driver's License (aka L's) would be the next order of business, and by obtaining my L's I would be finally eliminating a huge barrier, immobility would be put to rest. I would no longer be pinned down to the physical clutter of the house, but I could drive around the city or just chill in my ride. Tony and I took Driver's Education together on Salem Avenue at the infamous D&D Driving school.

50

D&D Driving School - Dayton, Ohio

D&D was the hoodest driving school in the area, but it was where all the black kids in the city who were hungry for their L's at sixteen had to go. My instructor once had me run all of her daily errands, including picking up her daughter from daycare, and taking her through the drive-thru at Burger King before we began our instruction time. But it all paid off in September 2004, only a few days after my 16th birthday. Grandpa Payne picked me up from school in his old school silver Mercedes and drove us to Huber Heights where I would pass my test on the first attempt. Grandpa had purchased a late 1970 diesel Mercedes from a woman at the church who was having a difficult financial time. He paid $5,000 for a loud, gas guzzling, rusted silver Mercedes that probably belonged at the local junk yard. It wasn't the most ideal vehicle to use for a driver's license test, it was bulky like a fullback, but I was in no position to be picky. After knocking out the test my next mission was to acquire a whip. So, I did some digging and stumbled on the Goodwill Auto Auction. I heard rumors of people getting nice cars for $300-$400 dollars, and non-running ones for around $100. I only had $100, but I prayed that I could get lucky and leave with a running vehicle. It was a

51

cold Saturday morning and it was extremely crowded. I remember the master of ceremony was speaking at an accelerated pace and it was hard to really make out what he was saying, "Do I hear $400, do I hear $300." I grew more and more anxious by his speaking pace and was afraid I might miss out on a deal, but the one thing I did know was that you had to yell your bid and not to bid more than you had in your pocket. As he was mcing the event some other guy would attempt to start the cars. Some vehicles would give out, some would smoke, and others just didn't start at all. It had got down to the last car, a dusty grey 1987 Ford Tempo, the same year I was born. They started the bid at $500, nobody said shit. The car was smoking but it started, and the engine didn't sound half bad, not that I knew much about cars, but it wasn't squealing like some of the others I had heard. "$100, for this running 1987 Ford tempo," "$100," I declared! "Sold," the auctioneer declared. I went into a trailer that was inside of the gated lot that enclosed the auction. I signed some paperwork, they took my $100, plus some fees for taxes. Thankfully Uncle Art covered the fees because I had no extra. They handed me the title and made me the happiest guy in all of Dayton that day. I could now drive around Dayton as much as my heart desired, and I was no longer a slave to the schedule of the RTA. Many nights that followed I would just sleep outside in my new ride. It wasn't the most comfortable, nor the safest place to sleep, but the peace of mind was priceless. I loved the fact that there weren't any roaches crawling on me while I slept, and no mice traps would go off throughout the night. I would just recline my seat, close my eyes, and envision better days.

My childhood kitchen

Senior Year of High School
2004-2005

"First came the bullshit, the drama wit my momma, she got on some fly

shit, so I split, and said that I'm a be that seed that doesn't need much

to succeed"

DMX - Slippin

Dec. 18, 2004

The worst day of my life occurred in the early morning of December 18, 2004. Gloria never stayed with us, even though all of her bull shit belongings were with us, but through some sort of cosmic intervention she did on the night of Dec.17, 2004. I think she told Grandma and I that Derrick had jumped on her, and she was going to be staying with us for a few days. She moved mountains of clothes that covered the bed in her childhood room, transferred them to the mountains of junk that surrounded the bed, and went to sleep. It was like she uncovered a treasure beneath the trash. I remember being frustrated that night because she found a way to sleep on a bed, even though my Grandma and I never did, because we weren't allowed to touch her things or enter any of the bedrooms. But on this day around 3am she woke me up, I responded, "What do you want", she replied, "It's your Grandpa we need to get to the hospital." I immediately lost my attitude and got dressed. As we pulled into the parking lot of Good Samaritan hospital Aunt Cynthia called her again, " Uh huh, awww, so he didn't make it," Gloria responded. I can remember looking at her and hoping I misinterpreted her responses to my Aunt. Gloria looked at me and said, "He didn't make it," I refused to believe it. I never cried so hard and for so long. It was as if every ounce of breath in my body had vanished, I wanted to jump right out of her Nissan and dive into the middle of traffic, I wanted to hurt her, because I felt she had no right to deliver the worst news I had ever received. Grandpa Payne was my best friend, and to be told he was dead from my worst enemy was pouring fresh salt onto an open wound. When Aunt Cynthia and Ali came outside from the hospital I immediately hopped in their car, I didn't even look at Gloria again. I now felt that I could mourn, I could allow the pain to take over my body. I didn't like the feeling of being weak in front of my enemy. Aunt Cynthia drove Ali and I to our Grandparents house, which was only 10 minutes away from the hospital. During the car ride none of us said a word, we were all too busy crying, he was the patriarch, the glue that bound us all together. As soon as we pulled up to Grandpa's house I was overtaken by another level of sadness. The home that held my hero, best-friend, and biggest advocate would never be the same. His voice, his smile, his smell, and his laugh were all infinitely tied to this house. As much pain as I felt, I knew that at least one person's heart was equally as shattered, my Grannie Payne. As we walked inside we noticed a bunch of people I had never seen before, or maybe I had, but I was too distraught to make out their faces. We hugged Grannie, she was broken, but you could tell that seeing two of her Grandsons was a much-needed jolt of love. We had all been delivered an unexpected blow, our leader had left us in the dark of the night. A heart attack claimed my Grandfather's life at the tinder age of 69.

Grandpa, Ali, and me

Coldest Winter Ever

"I cried so hard that my eyes bled three frozen lakes and gave birth to

the coldest winter ever"

Rudy Francisco - Shattered

We buried Grandpa in his hometown of Richmond, Virginia on Dec. 27, 2004. It was crazy for me to be in Virginia burying my Grandpa during the Christmas holiday, a time that was traditionally spent over his house, opening gifts, eating pancakes, and bonding with my family. When I returned to Dayton, I felt lost, my biggest cheerleader, strongest advocate, the man who welcomed me into his home from the day I was born, my hero, and my best friend, had been taken from me. Grandpa leaving this soon was not part of my life plan. We never had too many formal discussions about college or my future goals, but I knew that no matter what I did, he would be right by my side. A few weeks before he passed away, I remember Grannie Payne had sparked the conversation about post-high school plans, "ShoMari ain't going to nobody's college he don't do his work in high school," she said. "Actually, I plan to go to Western Kentucky University (WKU), and I'm going to cut hair in the dorms for spending money," I responded sarcastically. WKU had stopped by my high school once so it was the first college that came to mind when I was put on the spot. After Grandpa passed, we found a brand-new pair of Wahl clippers in his car, my final Christmas gift. I just knew that Grandpa would be with me for a very long time, and that it would be his wisdom that would carry me through college and throughout life. The next few weeks I cried nearly nonstop; I didn't want to talk to anyone. I would just lay on the floor and cry for hours.

He was a faithful servant of God at Zion Baptist Church, where he resided in Dayton. Minister Payne was a Sunday school teacher, a spirit- filled, devoted leader, having served on the Trustee Board and Deacon Board. At the time of his death, he was president of Men of Zion. He retired with 21 years of military service with the USAF and a retired civil servant of WPAFB. He was a member of Phi Beta Sigma Fraternity and the Edgar W. Dugger Military Lodge No. 123 PHA

CHAPTER VII
Freshman Orientation

A month after Grandpa passed away, I received an unexpected letter from Western Kentucky University welcoming me to campus. I absolutely couldn't believe it! I didn't know how I was going to pay for it, I had never been there before, but I knew this was where I was supposed to go. I knew Grandpa must have called in some favors because it truly was not in the cards for me to go to college. To confirm my admission, I was required to attend a freshman orientation, take a placement test, and visit campus, but I had no clue how I was going to get to Bowling Green, Kentucky. I didn't dare to ask my mom, but the death of Grandpa had given me the strength to ask my dad. I also needed to fill out something called a FAFSA. I asked Gloria if she could help me (since she was technically my custodial parent) and she said, "I ain't giving them people my information," and thought nothing else of it. So I estimated some numbers for her income and figured I'd let someone help me once I got there.

I can't remember the exact date, but it was a chilly Saturday morning, in February 2005, when Dad drove me down to Western Kentucky University for Freshman orientation. He seemed pretty shocked that I was doing anything positive with my life and felt compelled to sacrifice his time and make the drive. It was sort of a guilty confession in a sense, "Well damn somebody wants the boy I had nothing to do with raising, sold to the highest bidder," at least that's how I felt that he felt. Prior to Grandpa's passing, Dad and I hadn't spoke for three years prior, so the four-hour drive was extremely awkward. The last time we spent any significant time together I was 13 years old, and we got in a heated argument at Grandpa's house. We were in the kitchen having a shouting match and I remember opening the door to the garage to escape the chaos, Dad swiftly followed. The next thing I remember I was in the air, bracing myself in preparation for impact. Dad had launched me into the heavens, culminating with a thunderous second coming on the hood of Grannie Payne's 98 Buick Lesabre. I wasn't by definition a pipsqueak, and although Dad had seen all of the Bruce Lee movies, he wasn't necessarily known for his physical prowess, this feat was powered by something deeper, maybe regret, maybe anger, but whatever it was I felt every ounce of it. He could have easily walked past me and headed back to his life in Columbus, Ohio with his comfortable salary, lovely fiancé', and newly built 3-story home. But that's how my dad operates, he goes for blood, he wants you to remember his rage. This was the first time I had seen him embody so much violence and anger towards me, and I never really recovered from it. Later that evening Grandpa and Grannie Payne took me to Children's Hospital to get the knot on the back of my head examined, I think we told the medical staff that I had fallen while playing basketball. Dad never called to apologize or even to talk about what occurred, and at 13 years old it was a defining moment in our relationship.

A few years after the incident Grandpa suggested that I call Dad and make amends, "Be the bigger person ShoMari," I reluctantly conceded, and called the last number that I remembered. The phone rang and my stepmom Karma answered and joyfully handed Dad the phone after I revealed my identity. I was pissed that it was the right number. Dad sounded happy to talk to me which I found odd since he never once called or seemed interested in my existence after the slam. We saw each other a few times prior to Grandpa's passing, but it was nothing like our relationship before the vicious slam. Nonetheless, he drove me down for the required orientation, something that was outside of his normal character. I think the loss of Grandpa had a resounding effect on our broken relationship, he knew that had Grandpa still been alive he would have been the one taking me. Grandpa was truly the father I never had. During the orientation I was hit by a quiet reminder of how I had been forced to navigate through life alone. Dad was exhausted from the four-hour drive and opted to sleep in the car during the orientation. I figured maybe he'd sleep a few minutes then call when he was ready to join the rest of the parents and students. I remember checking my phone repeatedly and hovering around areas with ample cellular coverage to ensure I didn't miss his call. Four hours later I had completed my placement tests, learned some campus history, walked a full tour, and purchased a white Western Kentucky ball-cap from the campus bookstore (I wore that hat to school every day for the rest of my senior year). During the orientation I sunk into a quicksand of embarrassment. I watched as other parents asked challenging questions to the campus ambassadors, drilling them on WKU history, graduation rates, curriculum, scholarship packages, network of esteemed alumni, and the overall merits of the institution. Some parents seemed uneasy as the WKU representatives attempted to address their apprehensions, others seemed excited, one of mine was sleep in the car and the other could care less. I was used to being alone in Dayton, but I figured that for my college orientation things might be different, maybe I had finally earned his respect, love, and selflessness.

However, I quickly realized that this new journey called college was going to be all on me, similar to the 17 years prior, especially with no Grandpa Payne to cheer me on. The drive back to Dayton from WKU was even more awkward, we didn't speak much. He seemed pissed the orientation lasted four hours, and I was disappointed that I was the only prospective student without some visible support. I remember looking out the window of my Grandpa's old Mercedes when we drove by the University of Louisville, which was about the halfway mark of our trip. The campus had a certain jenesequa in comparison to WKU, in a disgruntled voice I heard, "Sheesh that school is closer why you ain't just go there, got me driving to Bowling Green, Kentucky." I just gave him a puzzled look, as if to say, "Do you think the University of Louisville would admit a minority student from a high-poverty, low-performing high school with a 1.3 GPA." He was unaware that my acceptance into WKU was accomplished through a testing miracle, and there weren't any more attractive options available for me to escape my environment.

Close the Deal

I managed to graduate high school by the hair on my chinny chin chin. Once I was accepted into WKU, not graduating from Jefferson High School was going to be the last thing to stop me from escaping my environment. I figured my teachers would cut me some slack since I was accepted into college, but that wasn't the case. I paraded my acceptance letter throughout school and pinned it on this board that our administrators created to highlight students going to college. Our Principal, Counselor, and Teachers were baffled by how the boy who barely ever came to school and was sitting on a 1.3 GPA was accepted into a decent college. I think the rumor was that I typed the letter myself. My high school English teacher Ms. Cook failed me for both junior and senior English, which was obviously a mandatory class. I was forced to sign up for correspondence in effort to get credit for those courses. Correspondence is a credit recovery program primarily for low performing students, it was a thick packet of curriculum that is shipped to you directly, requires you to complete 100% of the work, send back for grading, and earn a minimum of 80% to receive credit. I completed correspondence for junior & senior English. I managed to complete my Senior English packet in two weeks flat, and received a 90%, allowing me the privilege of graduating from Jefferson High School. Jefferson is one of the lowest ranked schools in the State, and I barely made it across that stage.

"Jefferson Twp. ranked last in the state in four-year graduation rate, at

50 percent. No other district in Ohio was below 65 percent"

Jeremy Kelly - Dayton Daily News

Things started coming together for me, I was accepted into college, and would soon be able to escape the place that was the root of my pain. A handful of years earlier, Grandpa had purchased my older sister LaKisha a 1996 Ford Contour when she first moved to Dayton from Lansing, Michigan, a car she returned to him when she upgraded in 2003. Grannie Payne signed over the Contour to me shortly after Grandpa passed, which was truly a blessing. My 87 Tempo had given out on me after about a year, and my Astro Van only lasted a few months. The summer before I left for college I barely spent any time at Grandma Clark's, I was either with my best friend Shawn at his spot in Englewood, Ohio, or over Grannie Payne's helping her prepare the house for sale, a decision she made after Grandpa passed.

CHAPTER VII
WKU Freshman Year
Fall 2005 - Spring 2006

"As a child I dreamed about a bed day and night, fantasized over it, and eventually it manifested. Looking back, it's easy to see that a fifty-dollar twin size bed should not have been the highest aim of a child for 17 years."

ShoMari Payne - Dreaming

I never saw the sun shine as bright as it did on the day I left for college. I remember the process of preparing my things for departure. Prior to packing up my rubber maids I diligently shook all four or five of my shirts outside and sat my TV outside in the garage for several days because roaches would often climb into the openings in the back of the TV, and crawl across the screen while I was watching a show. I refused to carry any roaches, clothes that had been chewed on, or rat feces with me on my new journey. I didn't have much to bring, a few fitted hats, couple of oversized polos and a pair of grey Nike huaraches made the cut. Unknowingly, what I did carry to the beautiful campus of Western Kentucky University was a luggage full of bad habits and a learned culture of failure. Prior to my mediocre ACT score, I hadn't achieved anything significant academically since the third grade. I wasn't equipped with essential habits that make for a first-generation college student success story. Positive habits like study skills, discipline, time management, networking, and campus engagement were all absent in my bag of goodies. But unlike high school, this time around I would not be defined by being dusty, broke, and poor. I would do whatever it took to fill my closet with gear, and obtain the necessary medical attention needed for my Hyperhidrosis condition.

habit
: a usual way of behaving : something that a person does often in a regular and repeated way.

High on the priority list was securing a job to support myself and acquiring all of the material things that I never had. I was motivated to find a new identity, whether that meant working at Cracker Barrel for $8.50/hour or stealing from the local mall, I was determined not to relive my childhood experience. I would no longer run to the bus stop early to shake cockroaches out of my backpack before other students arrived. No more wearing the same shirt 3-4x in one week. No more sleeping on the floor and denying friends access to my dwelling, I was motivated to obtain what I felt was normality.

65

"I can let you check the tag now I'm rocking name brand"
Drake - Look Alive

As a freshman at WKU my class schedule wasn't that intense; an introductory business course, English 101, African-American studies, and a Physical Education class, but for some reason the most difficult feat in the world was physically getting out of my bed and going to class. Maybe it was because I never had a bed, but somewhere deep down I knew that I was a fraud and had no business being in college. I knew that I had not invested as much academically as other students, and this was evident upon my first day of class. I knew that if I was presented with an obvious question in class that I would have not the slightest clue how to answer. I remember going to my Psychology class during the first week and being completely overwhelmed by the sheer size of the class, let alone the content. I had never sat down with my parents and mapped out a college or career plan, and I never promised my Grandma that I would get her out of poverty, I just wanted to be free, and I finally was. This was the result of an ACT score and a 4-hour drive that I would never hear the end of, "Who the one who drove you down to that school," my dad would often utter as his sole investment in my college education. I soon realized that my class schedule had been created long before I stepped foot on campus. It really looked more like this.

ShoMari Payne

Western Kentucky University
Term: Fall 2005
Major - Marketing (Seeking Admission)

Mice & Roaches	17 years (3 Credit hours)
Empty Stomach	17 years (3 Credit hours)
Sleeping on the floor	17 years (3 Credit hours)
Dreaming of a bed	17 years (3 Credit hours)
Class Clown	13 years (3 Credit hours)

"What we stare at, we become"
Unknown

The college dream for me was truthfully the college dormitory. For a boy who called the floor his bed for seventeen years, the experience of college was beyond anything I had ever conceptualized. My vision never stretched beyond the level of bare necessity, I never envisioned becoming a CEO, CFO, or head of marketing for a Fortune 500 company. I chose to major in Business because my High School Accounting teacher pulled me aside after learning of my college acceptance, "You need some structure, choose Business," and I didn't disagree. I wasn't groomed in a household of rules, discipline, or structure, and I knew nothing about saving money, building wealth, or which button I should press on the elevator towards economic prosperity. I was a maximum award receiving Pell Grant student from a low socioeconomic background that attended a failing public school district my entire life. So, I rationalized that majoring in business was indeed a logical decision, and I certainly didn't believe I was cut out to be in engineering or medicine. I wasn't the kid contemplating a career in marine biology at age 12, and I never researched information on career trajectories, median salaries, or completed a basic personality assessment to determine my strengths and weaknesses. I wasn't familiar

67

with career resource databases like the Bureau of Labor Statistics, O'Net, or Vault that I use with my students at Sinclair Community College. I bet it all on a twin size bed at WKU with a roommate from Illinois named Kyle, who sacrificed showers for the trendy new AXE body spray, I remember suffocating in our dorm from the smell and would spray some of his cans out the window when he left for class. Was this my destiny? A twin sized bed in a 100 sq. ft room, a major picked from a hat by my high school accounting teacher, and a 17-year-old boy primed to waste thousands of dollars in financial aid? Or was this just the manifestation of 17 years of continuous expectancy? The Universe will always partner with you when it determines that you are serious about your desires. And during that interval in my life I was dead serious about one thing, rising from the floor.

"Why did people live so long content with the horse and carriage and not enjoy the automobile? Because they couldn't imagine it. Their minds were not trained to demand such a thing"
Raymond Holliwell

Habits

"The chains of life are too light to be felt, until they are too heavy to be broken"

Warren Buffett

When I first arrived on campus, I struggled mightily to defeat the demons of my past, but the stimulus (pain) just wasn't there anymore. For once in my life I had everything that I ever wanted. A meal plan with access to fresh food at my beckoning call, a mini-fridge full of Powerade and lunchables, clean clothes, no roaches, no mice, no more sleeping on the cold hard floor, air conditioning in the summer, heat in the winter, an abundance of girls, and most importantly a bed. There was no reason (stimulus) to stretch beyond this new level, I had arrived.

68

Inviting girls over to my dorm room at Keen Hall to watch movies on my 19-inch fatback television was one of the highlights of my freshman year. Mainly because growing up no one ever stepped foot inside my house due to the severity of the hoarding, and the protection of the family secret. In college it was refreshing to invite company over to my 100 sq. ft shared palace. I finally had a place to call my own, but my priorities were completely out of whack. When the semester began, I never made my way to the campus library, I'm not even positive I knew where it was located, but somehow I routinely found my way to the campus Rec Center aka Preston, the dining halls, and the computer lab for some good ole Facebook time.

"Actions express priorities"
Mahatma Gandhi

At what point did I plan to accept some personal accountability? I didn't comprehend the reality that my opportunity was right there, a moment in time I could never touch again. Compared to my life back in Dayton, college was nirvana. I was in love with every aspect of college besides waking up, going to class, studying, and turning in assignments. But when my first semester grades posted I was slightly taken aback by my inability to garner a 2.0.

Western Kentucky University
Institution Credit
Term: Fall 2005
Major: Marketing (Seeking Admission)

African American Experience - 3 credit hours	C
University Experience Business - 2 credit hours	C
Business & Professional Speaking - 3 credit hours	D
Intro to College Writing - 3 credit hours	C
Fundamentals of Movement - 2 credit hours	F

Overall GPA 1.66

But what I really wasn't expecting was the email that followed.

Subject: Academic Probation
Dear: Shomari Payne
You have been placed on Academic Probation. If you do not earn above a 2.0 for the Spring 2006 Semester you will be dismissed from the University.

I was convinced there had been a mistake, and I didn't understand why this was an issue. You mean you can get kicked out of college? This was news to me. I wanted to reply, "You can keep getting my financial aid, let's just all chill out and keep the good times rolling, please don't end this dream come true for me." The Spring Semester 2006 provided

70

me with one more opportunity to get it right academically, earn above a 2.0 GPA, and avoid academic suspension. When the Spring 2006 semester began, I was $1,500 short on tuition, the IRS probably ran the numbers on the phony information I provided on my FAFSA, but without that $1,500 I was to be sent home within two weeks. I picked up the phone and pleaded with Grandma Clark, hoping she may have magically saved $1,500 dollars in her pocketbook for a rainy day. "Grandma they trying to kick me out of college, I need $1,500 this is some bull shit." I conveniently left out the email regarding my probationary status or my plan beyond the Spring 2006. Looking back, I see the selfishness in my spirit, leaving her in the oppression, and asking for money so that I would not have to return to it. Grandma held onto the southern morals and the aspirations she cultivated while she and her siblings dodged projectiles from prejudice white students who passed them on the school bus as they walked. She firmly believed in the power of education; she knew it was the vehicle to a better life. Maybe it was because her Grandmother was a slave and received the punishment of having her hands cut off for teaching other slaves how to write. Or maybe it was because she saw her potential in me. She had no clue I was goofing around, sleeping in, skipping class, and chasing women. She could have used that $1,500 dollars to rent an apartment, or pay a delinquent bill, but instead I heard her smile all the way from Kentucky, as if to say, " I won't let you down grandson." We hung up the phone and she made a couple of calls on my behalf. She called back a few hours later, "Between your Aunt Mildred, Aunt Doll, Aunt Esther, and me, we've got the $1,500." I honestly couldn't believe it; this was exactly what I needed to stay in school. She informed me that she would give the money to my mom so that she could pay my outstanding tuition online. "Gloria said she can take care of everything on the computer," I hesitated, "Grandma do not give the money to her, just put it in my account and I can pay it in person," I responded. "No no no baby we

71

want to make sure your college is paid, you might get this money and spend it on something else, this is for ya tuition," she said. As you can guess, the money never reached me or my outstanding account balance. Grandma's blind faith in her eldest daughter has always been the bane of her existence. I later discovered that Gloria enjoyed a nice vacation with Derrick on my behalf. She said that when she went to pay the balance online it was actually $1,700, and since we were short on the balance she used the money as a loan to herself. Thankfully WKU allowed me to stay in the dorms until the semester ended, and I received Withdraws (W's) in all my classes. I returned back to Dayton in May 2006 with 12 credit hours and a 1.6 GPA, and in the blink of an eye my life's fortune was snatched from beneath me. Something I prayed over for seventeen years had vanished, and I was back in west Dayton with the roaches and the rats.

Western Kentucky University
Institution Credit
Term: Spring 2006
Major: Marketing (Seeking Admission)

Intro Chemistry - 3 credit hours	W
Intro Economics - 3 credit hours	W
Intermediate Algebra - 3 credit hours	W
Intro Psychology - 3 credit hours	W
Introductory Sociology - 3 credit hours	W

CHAPTER VIII
Summer 2006 - *Back to Reality*

I arrived back in Dayton in May 2006, returning with a few more muscles than when I left. This was primarily due to my personal commitment to the campus Rec Center, and access to nutritious meals at the exquisite campus dining halls. My first priority upon returning to Dayton was to get some wheels. I knew that getting back to WKU would require me to make some serious money over the summer. After a few weeks I managed to scrape up enough cash to buy a Caprice Classic from my cousin Kendra's boyfriend for $500 bucks. I remember being pissed that he wouldn't sell it for any lower. I don't remember how I managed to salvage $500 dollars, but I was always good at borrowing money. On the day of the purchase I caught the bus to meet her boyfriend at the title office, I remember being pissed that he put down the actual sale price for the car, which forced me to pay even more money to the State. This was a no-no in the hood, you always put $0 for the sale price, and say that it was a gift. Feeling ripped off by the whole ordeal I hopped in his whip with a slight attitude as he drove us to the location of the Caprice. We pull up and I immediately notice this was not the same Caprice I remembered from before I left for college. The paint was now two colors, white and maroon, and not in a cool two-tone sort of way, but from rust and deterioration. I immediately had that feeling in my stomach that I had made a grave mistake and was tempted to ask for a refund. "You might want to get that radiator checked too, and the first place you need to go is the gas station." I received the keys, started her up, and sped up Gettysburg in my new Caprice, (speeding down Gettysburg is a rite of passage in Dayton). I knew there was no way the Caprice would make the journey to WKU, but maybe I could save up enough to buy something better once I found a job. While pumping gas at the Shell on Gettysburg and Germantown I happened to look across the street at Papa John's, and the now hiring sign stood out like a sore thumb. I filled out the application and to my surprise received an on the spot interview. I was expecting a much more thorough screening process, but the oversized African-American manager whose name escapes me asks just one sole question, "Do you have reliable transportation," I took a deep swallow and answered, "Aw yea I just bought a car, I'm good there." I landed the job on the spot and would soon begin delivering pizzas at the most dangerous Papa John's location in the city at the corner of Gettysburg and Germantown.

Germantown & Gettysburg intersection - Dayton, Ohio

My first problem was the car itself, which required that in addition to pizzas and 2-liters, I also carry five or six jugs of water in the backseat to pour into the radiator after every delivery. The smell of radiator fluid and engine smoke preceded my coming. I remember delivering pizzas to Tony's house while he was having a small get-together. I begged my boss not to make me do that run, but he insisted. I pulled up as incognito as my smoking engine would allow, but the homies were already posted outside. Tony tried to hold back his laugh and just said, "Man had I know it was you I would have had a better tip," we gave dap and I departed back to Papa John's. But the biggest problem with this job wasn't running into friends, or the condition of my Caprice, it was being robbed at gunpoint for tips and large pizzas. I remember once delivering to a house that appeared to be a bando (abandoned). The screen door was shut but the main door was wide open. I announced myself, "Papa John's Pizza," she responded, "Come on in baby I don't bite." I ignored the first rule of robbery prevention training and stepped inside. The shower was running, and I assumed she would be coming out shortly to pay me and allow me to get on my way. Instead the next thing I felt was the steel against my back, "Drop the pizzas baby, you got any money on ya." She tapped my back-side and retrieved my wallet out of my company issued khakis. She confiscated $26 dollars and told me not to worry about calling the police because this wasn't even her house. Later that summer I was robbed on the fourth of July, it was the late shift and I was having trouble finding the right apartment. I slowed down and began squinting for addresses, and out of nowhere, "Pow Pow Pow." I slammed the brakes, put my Chevy in park, and ran out as fast as I could! When I looked back, I saw four teenagers walking away from my Caprice with the pizzas, including the protective heat wave bag. They had thrown firecrackers through my passenger window, but I thought it was gunshots. My manager saw the disappointment on my face when I returned, but he didn't care, he sent me to another round of robbery prevention training. It was truly a reality check being back in Dayton that summer.

Most of my friends did not leave Dayton for college or the military, and that summer I could feel the weight of post-high school life already starting to unfold in our endeavors. Many of our star athletes had already returned to the city for good, trading Division II basketball and football scholarships for selling narcotics, budding rap careers, or both. "That had us running too much, I said fuck this shit and quit," a good friend said regarding leaving his football scholarship on the table. Other friends thought professional sports was the only way out of the jungle and took Rec League games at the YMCA to a whole new level. I remember that summer going to hoop at the downtown YMCA and there was a 2-hour wait to get on the court. Dayton hoop star Daequan Cook who was one of the best high school players in the nation was casually shooting around before heading off to Ohio State University, and eventually a solid NBA career. That day everyone wanted to get on the court to prove they were also NBA material. One cat pulled out what had to be $10,000 in cash and started offering hundred-dollar bills to move up in line for the next game. Being home that summer was a small snippet into the life that was awaiting if I stayed. The poverty in my life, and in my community affected me deeper this time around because I had finally seen and experienced something different. I was motivated not to allow my first-year failure in college to define my academic future or potential. I knew that if I could get back to college, I would relish the opportunity.

The same fire that cooks your food can burn your house down, how will you use your pain?

As the summer waned it looked less and less likely I was going to be able to afford a return to college. I owed a sizable balance to WKU, and even if I hadn't gotten robbed for tips, my $6.25/hour just wasn't adding up quick enough. Doubt and depression poured into my thoughts and it became increasingly difficult to convince myself I had the intellectual ability or finances to thrive on a college campus. Soon the lonely nights of delivering pizzas got longer and longer, and I began to question when did life U-turn so quickly? Three months ago, I was waking up at noon on a beautiful campus, shooting hoops at the Preston Rec Center, and walking to the campus Fresh Food Market for an early afternoon breakfast. Now I was back on the floor next to my all too familiar friends, the roaches and rats. I felt like the biggest failure, frustrated that I didn't take advantage of my opportunity to escape this life. Was this my natural state of existence? Was I predestined to this lifelong sentence with poverty and oppression? Did I let Gloria defeat me? I would ask myself these questions daily. Like someone struggling with any addiction, I had allowed the power of habit to carry me from the residence halls of a beautiful southern campus to the all too familiar struggles of the inner city. My twin size bed at Keen hall was everything I had ever dreamed of. It was much more inviting than my cold hard pallet back in Dayton next to the cockroaches and mice, and subsequently more inviting than an 8:00am psychology class. During that time, I wasn't aware of the immense power of visualization, from which my new reality had stemmed. I had wasted so much of my mental energy as a child on something that really wasn't that important, having my own bed, but to me it was the most important thing in the world. I had fell for a mirage, a smoke screen. Seventeen years of dreaming was not used preparing for my release from oppression, but only wishing for upgrades to my circumstances. I never saw myself beyond the floor. If you have ever been to a prison, you will see two different types of prisoners. You will find inmates like Malcolm X, those who have committed to the task of developing themselves daily, sharpening their mind and body, diligently preparing for the day when they can once again inhale the sweet air of freedom. In Malcolm X's autobiography he made this proclamation eluding to his childhood, education, and time in prison.

"I finished the eighth grade in Mason, Michigan. My high school was the black ghetto of Roxbury, Massachusetts. My college was in the streets of Harlem, and my master's was taken in prison"

Malcolm X

On the opposite end of the spectrum you will find those prisoners who have succumbed to the prison mentality and engage in deviant behavior that breeds violence and survival. These individuals carry with them the mentality that led them to this mental and physical prison. I was of the latter, I had become stagnant, complacent, and I was no longer producing results, thus I had ceased the powerful process of creation. I was experiencing mental atrophy. Let's go back to where it all started, where I accumulated the mind state that derailed my potential. Back to my hometown of Dayton, Ohio, where for seventeen long years I built the identity of failure and a minimized my vision of myself. Where mountains of trash and fleets of cockroaches had circumcised my hope and ransacked my highest aspirations.

Where Grandma and I slept

It's over, yeah it's over yeah, I'm leaving, I'm gone
I can't stay here no more and I can't sleep on the floor
Man, I'm leaving, I'm leaving, you know I got my reasons
Yeah I'm leaving, yeah I'm leaving, yeah I'm leaving, I'm gone
I'm leaving, I'm gone
I had to knock down the wall
Yeah I swear to God that I'm gone
I'm leaving, I'm leaving
No looking back when I'm gone
Drake - Now and Forever

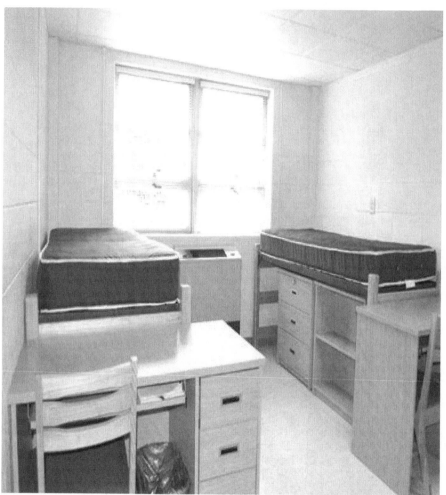

My first bed - Keen Hall, Western Kentucky University

ACT II
THE INNER CITY

*"If I were giving a young man advice as to how he might succeed in life,
I would say to him pick out a good father and mother and begin life in
Ohio"*

Wilbur Wright

*"In this America millions of people find themselves living in rat-infested
vermin filled slums"*

Dr. Martin Luther King Jr.

Dayton, Ohio is the quintessential blue-collar midwestern city, unique in opportunities relative to geography and hue. In 2017, Dayton landed 15th on the list of the most segregated cities in the U.S. For African-Americans concentrated on the disinvested west-side, we face a murder rate rivaling larger cities like Chicago, Illinois. As children, we are shuttled through underfunded school systems, raised predominantly by Grandparents, and exposed to the ugliest sides of society prematurely. Very few family businesses or heirlooms are passed down, rather we inherited systemic joblessness, coupled with the gaping absence of parental support. I have lost relatives to both drug addiction and the drug war and stood helplessly as mass incarceration has ripped through my city, leaving behind debris of broken families and abandoned homes. I've shed tears witnessing childhood friends graduate from the playground only to gravitate towards the graveyard. If there are advantages for growing up in areas like west Dayton with little support, they are buried in the lower chambers of one's self, and rarely found by the possessor. The reality of growing up black and disadvantaged is a childhood filled with anger, academic frustration, and systemic criminalization. Journey with me inside the black-hole called the inner-

81

city, hear the stories closest to me, learn of my personal heroes who migrated North to escape Jim Crow, domestic terrorism, and economic scarcity. Meet some of my childhood friends, students, mentors, and victims. ACT I focused on my personal experience growing up poor and disadvantaged. Chapter II chronicles my growth in knowledge of the world around me, and my ever-developing understanding of the global plot that sought to destroy me, and people like me.

"O afflicted city, lashed by storms and not comforted, I will build you

with stones of turquoise, your foundations with sapphires"

Isaiah 54:11

CHAPTER I
Dayton, Ohio

As a boy, growing up in Dayton, Ohio provided me with no true sense of pride. I was unaware of the city's unique place in American history and didn't really care to learn. Like every other kid from Dayton, I was taught that we held claim to the infamous Wright Brothers, but was not sure why they were so important, I had never boarded an airplane, nor been to the Dayton International Airport. From my perspective, I only saw the struggle connected to the inner-city, the families waiting on the 6:30pm RTA line-up downtown, and the desperation on the faces of those who missed this almost festive event. Every evening at 6:30, you could find every bus in the city downtown, positioned on all four corners of Main and Third street, waiting to take passengers in all directions across the city. If you missed 6:30 line up, you had to wait until the next line-up at 7:30, which had significantly less busses, and a much longer ride to your destination, filled with what I felt were "off the books" employee breaks. Returning home from part-time jobs at McDonalds and Fazoli's, I missed the 6:30 line-up many nights, and that intersection always seemed to get dark by 6:40. Some nights I just preferred hanging out downtown, instead of rushing home just to sleep on the floor. You would see some fiends, some dope boys, some tricks, but as long as you didn't look like a "Chauncey" nobody would try you. So, I'd stand around draped in an all-white tall tee that I wore beneath my McDonalds polo, sticker still hugged against my chest, sit back, and just observe.

What I did know about the makeup of my city was that a disproportionate number of homes were abandoned on the black side, and the stores that Grandma and I frequented were all slowly going out of business. Ren's Supermarket in Jefferson Township closed when I was about three years old, then the Kroger's on Gettysburg closed, followed by the McDonald's on Gettysburg and Germantown, the Salem Mall in Trotwood was demolished, then the Cub Foods store in Trotwood's Consumer Square closed, and finally the Walmart in Trotwood. Most recently the Aldi's in Westtown closed, effectively creating a food desert in the area.

Kroger - Gettysburg Avenue, Dayton, Ohio.

I learned about Brown vs. Board of Education but was unaware that the U.S public school systems remained largely segregated after that landmark case. I attended the same predominately black school district that Gloria, Uncle Art, and both of my aunts had attended, and although the district's name was the same, the byproduct was vastly different. Majority of the large factories equipped to employ low-skill laborers had vanished. What remained for the underclass in Dayton was just a handful of fast-food restaurants, and if you were really lucky, a retail job 20 minutes south in the affluent side of town. The economic decline of Dayton and other Rust-Belt cities is largely attributable to the loss of manufacturing jobs in the region. At its apex following World War II, Dayton was as important to the U.S economy as Silicon Valley is today. In addition to the Wright Brothers, Dayton gave birth to inventors like John H. Patterson, who invented the Cash Register and founded National Cash Register (NCR). Dayton's climate sparked entrepreneurs like Charles Kettering, and Fortune 500 companies such as Mead Paper Company. In 1900 Dayton claimed more patents per capita than any other city in the U.S. Dayton held the largest concentration of General Motors (GM) employees outside of its Michigan headquarters. Dayton was the 40th largest city in the U.S in 1940, and its population peaked in 1960 at around 260,000 people. Today the urban centre has lost over 100,000 residents, while the suburban population has grown exponentially. In 1930, 74% of Montgomery County's population lived in Dayton, today that number is less than a third. As of 2018 less than 20% of the Dayton metropolitan population has a Dayton zip code.

K-12 Public Schools

"They sending letters home from school, nobody read mine"
T.I - Still Ain't Forgave Myself

"Low poverty high schools have a culture of preparing students for prestigious PWIs. Whereas high poverty schools in the inner city have quite the opposite culture crisis."
Jack Schneider

Nights that should have been spent sitting at a desk studying, I spent standing on the couch terrified, watching rats scurry back and forth across the kitchen floor. My environmental conditions did me no favors when I arrived at school. The hoarding, cold nights on the floor, hungry nights, the cockroaches, the rats, and the impact on my self-esteem were factors that I was keenly aware of, and vehemently despised. But what was happening to me was much deeper than my physical oppression, and over time, I subsequently found it extremely difficult to pay attention in school, even when I did try my best. I remember the first time I was introduced to fractions in the second grade at Blairwood elementary. I was having difficulty wrapping my mind around the numerator/denominator concept, but soon fractions became an incomprehensible concept to grasp, while just a year prior I was tutoring multiplication for my peers after-school. In the social sciences I was no longer retaining the key takeaways from the required readings, was finding it increasingly difficult to focus, and began to challenge the institution of learning with my wit and ability to make others laugh. I could no longer distinguish verbs from adjectives, and progressively quit caring. I subconsciously began to see my school for the system it was and made it a daily ritual to disrespect that system. I no longer found pride in learning, and became fueled by the applause of my peers, when I habitually disrespected our underpaid teachers. I was constantly sent to the Principal's office, sent home, told not to return, and intentionally skipped. My behavioral issues at school did not manifest until around the second and third grade, but from there they spiraled into an uncontrollable fire. No adult was available to discipline me for my deviant behavior, and the lack of consequences or concern from a parent just added confidence to my ability to push the envelope.

Basic necessities such as dental, vision, and health care were not easily accessible due to a combination of factors, including Grandma never earning her driver's license, the restrictive schedule of the RTA, and a lack of access to my identification documents that Gloria kept out of our reach. I realized that I was having trouble seeing the chalkboard at school, even when I sat in the front row. I pleaded for Gloria to take me to the optometrist, but she rarely even attempted to fit me into her schedule. "ShoMari I work in Columbus, damn I can't wait till you start

85

driving," I remember she said to me as a 12-year-old. Yet I remember her stopping by showing us photo collages from her adventures with Derrick, illustrious cruises, Luther Vandross concerts, Kem concerts, Ron Isley concerts, trips to Vegas, plays downtown, sporting events, out of state festivals, the black expo, Bahamas, cruises, and many other fancy gala's. That's when I realized that Grandma and I were not only below Derrick in her hierarchy of importance, we were also below here piles of trash that she kept at our house. At school, comedy was the outlet I chose to cope with the pain and oppression.

"Those who are required to live in congested and rat-infested homes are aware that others are not so dehumanized. Young people in the ghetto are aware that other young people have been taught to read, that they have been prepared for college, and can compete successfully for white-collar, managerial, and executive jobs."

Kenneth Clarke

School Bus Rides

The school bus was always a journey onto itself. Many fights that came to pass on the school bus were planned during the school day. Some kids would hop on different buses to go over friends' houses, meet up for some risqué activities, or to avoid a pending confrontation, but the administrators tried to crack down on this practice, and unless you had written permission, you were told to ride your designated bus home. My bus from 5-12th grade was bus #19, which picked up all the kids in my neighborhood, a few kids on the rural streets, and route 4 (Germantown Pike) before heading to school or home. We had the identity of being one of the worse buses in the entire district. I rode the bus with a few of my good friends, Torrey, Demaris, and Shawn, so I was never too worried about getting my ass beat, but you never knew for certain what might happen if one of the Juniors or Seniors who usually drove happened to get on the bus. Torrey and Demaris lived across the street from one another, so I hung out over both of their houses a lot. I would get off the bus at Torrey's and we would go play basketball over Demaris house. Demaris was tough, he was raised by his dad and they owned upwards of ten pit bulls, no exaggeration. I remember his dad yelling at him and his little brother Dante', "Y'all niggas stop hooping and go feed them damn dogs now!" Dante' was tough too, and I think he could sense that I couldn't fight, so he would always try to size me up, wrestle, or slap box, even though I was three grades older. One morning freshman year I hopped on the bus, gave Torrey some dap, then I went to shake Dante's hand, but out of nowhere he slapped the shit out of me. Everyone on the bus oooooed in suspense to see what I was going to do. He was in sixth grade, but it was definitely a grown man slap to the face, so I pushed him against the school bus window. Demaris saw me push Dante' and began walking towards me from the back of the bus, "You pushed my little brother nigga," I responded, "He slapped me bruh." Demaris asked Dante' who denied hitting me. Demaris thought about it for a second, then cocked back his right arm, leaned in for a haymaker, and stopped right before his fist hit my face. I jumped back, "Bitch ass nigga don't ever touch my little brother," he said with disdain. Demaris and I were both written up and given Saturday School for the encounter. The next Saturday we served our sentence and didn't speak the entire time. The beef only lasted a few weeks, we want back way too far to hold onto a grudge.

A nigga never been as broke as me, I like that

When I was young I had two pair of Lees, besides that

The pinstripes and the gray

The one I wore on Mondays and Wednesdays

While niggas flirt, I'm sewing tigers on my shirt

And alligators

Ya wanna see the inside, huh, I see ya later

Here come the drama, oh, that's that nigga wit the fake, blaow!

Why you punch me in my face, stay in ya place

Notorious BIG

Saturday School

I was assigned to Saturday school almost every weekend throughout my first three years of high school. Saturday School was a 4-hour confinement in the shop classroom from 8:00 am to noon and was intended as punishment for at-risk students and deviant students like me. Not sure if they thought it through or maybe they did, but grouping the most disruptive students in the school together in one room for four hours turned out to be highly unproductive. We threw paper balls, watched TV, talked on the phone, had verbal altercations followed by physical altercations, and some students broke into classrooms and appropriately adjusted their failing grades in the gradebooks. Sometimes guys would pretend they needed to use the bathroom and meet up with a girl in an unlocked classroom. I never planned to drop-out or fail out of high school, but I allowed my circumstances at home to dictate my academic effort, so I walked the dangerous tightrope of academic dismissal. For me, living in poverty, meant living only for the moment, and many of my peers felt the same way. I coasted along the path of academic frustration for majority of high school and accepted this drift as my natural state of existence.

"Living in the projects, grew up with no lights on"
Tupac Shakur

CHAPTER II
Algebra I

I hadn't learned or retained anything mathematically from 4th-8th grade, but here I was sitting in a high school Algebra class freshman year without any of the requisite foundational skills. But instead of facing my deficiencies, I chose to disrupt the learning process by telling jokes while Mr. Allen was trying his best to teach. Mr. Allen was an ex-marine, a tall slender older white guy who didn't take no shit, his tolerance for my shenanigans was much lower than our other teachers. If I was clowning in Biology, Ms. Snyder would either stop teaching, or just tell the entire class to read the book. When I was clowning in Honors English freshman year, Mr.Phillips would just isolate my desk to the corner of the room. If I wasn't telling jokes, I was skipping class, anything was better than facing the embarrassment of my mounting academic deficiencies. I vividly remember Mr. Allen frequently walking over to the buzzer after I had accomplished the goal of distracting my peers, "Sending Shawn and ShoMari down to the office again." On one occasion, Mr. Allen looked me straight in the eye and said with a stone-cold voice, "Son, some people take Algebra II, but you my friend will take Algebra twice." I proved him a liar, I took Algebra I across the span of three separate academic years, first as a freshman, again as sophomore, and lastly during summer school at Wayne High School before heading into my junior year. Shawn failed Algebra twice as well and passed on his third attempt via correspondence. Shawn was my best-friend in high school, which came about through sheer admiration for one another's struggle. Shawn came from a single-parent home and caught the RTA from his house on the northwest side of Dayton at 4:00am, just arrive to his Grandpa's house in my neighborhood by 6:00am. We knew each other in middle school, but freshman year we really clicked and became partners in crime. Shawn didn't come from money, and his mom, Mrs. Karen, worked long hours to ensure that Shawn and his little sister had food on the table, and more opportunities than she had growing up. When Mrs. Karen worked double shifts, Shawn would let me spend the night during the week, and after school we would catch the RTA from my neighborhood back to his, which was counterproductive since I lived in much closer proximity to our school. I remember one night I stayed over Shawn's and I accidently left the mayonnaise out on the counter after making myself a sandwich, I pretended to be sleep while Ms. Karen cussed Shawn smooth out over the ordeal. Shawn never asked why he wasn't allowed inside my house, but he always opened his home to me, that made him my brother.

I remember we would cut class, my teachers used to hate me

The only reason that I did that was to keep from goin' crazy

I didn't give a damn 'bout my grades

That's probably why we failed the ninth grade

Me and my dawg, like it or not, we came out okay

Brent Faiyaz

Geometry

I can remember finally graduating to Geometry as a junior, in a melting pot classroom that blended high achieving freshman, with frustrated juniors and seniors. In Geometry I shared the crown of most feared joker with Mike and Tyre, they were what you would call "cool gangsters." They always had the latest gear, served time at even rougher schools than Jefferson, and were known for their ability to clown you in an instant. One particular day in Geometry stands out among the rest. Our teacher was attempting to go over a lesson, but everyone was focused on the conversation Mike and Tyre were having about the latest pair of Jordan's that were set to be released. They began describing the unique colors and detailed plans on how to pair them with specific outfits. I was knee-deep into one of those automobile sales magazines you grab on your way out of the grocery store, dreaming of one day owning a 2003 Dodge Durango and driving it to school. Tyre came over to my desk, snatched my magazine, raised it in the air and asked rhetorically, "What the hell you lookin at broke ass nigga, you ain't never gon be able to afford no damn car," the entire class laughed uncontrollably. As a lame attempt for a comeback, I reached into my pocket and pulled out my brand-new driver's license, the class was in awe (having your L's was one a status symbol, you were practically an adult). By this time our Geometry teacher, a middle-aged white guy who

91

I believe was a long-term substitute, had grown discouraged with the excessive talking and chose to retire to his desk, he might have even asked to glance at my auto magazine. This was a typical day in Geometry, cats talking about stealing clothes from the mall, the release date of the new Jordan's, shooting jokes at one another, watching basketball highlights and music videos on the three computers in the back of the room, and gossiping about who's sleeping with who. We found pride in frustrating our teachers until they reached their breaking point, the point of exhaustion, all in an effort to enjoy that interval of time unto ourselves. Looking back, I can see the years of frustration upon my teacher's faces. They knew what awaited for us.

"They knew the ground was trip-wired."
Ta-Nahesi Coates

ShoMari Payne

JEFFERSON HIGH SCHOOL	PAYNE, SHOMARI	STUDENT ID: 3415
2701 S. UNION ROAD	1550 KIMMEL LN	SEX: M
		BIRTHDATE:
DAYTON, OH 45418	DAYTON, OH 45418	ADMISSION DATE: 09/22/87
(937) 835-5691		WITHDRAWAL DATE:
JEFFERSON LOCAL SCHOOLS		08/01/01 / /
SCH CODE 361815		/ / / /
		GRADUATED ON: 05/24/05

ATTENDANCE:

				CREDIT			
YEAR	GRADE	COURSE TITLE	GPA S1 S2	FINAL	ATTM	EARN	SCHOOL

SCHOOL	DAYS	DAYS	TIMES
YEAR	PRESENT	ABSENT	TARDY

COURSE HISTORY

YEAR	GRADE	COURSE TITLE	GPA	S1	S2	FINAL	ATTM	EARN	SCHOOL
01/02	09	2 ALGEBRA I	Y		D	D	0.500	0.500	JFHIGH
01/02	09	2 CONCERT BAND	Y		B	B	0.500	0.500	JFHIGH
01/02	09	2 HONRS 103	Y		D	D	0.500	0.500	JFHIGH
01/02	09	2 INT SCIENCE	Y		C	C	0.500	0.500	JFHIGH
01/02	09	2 PHYS ED	Y		B	B	0.250	0.250	JFHIGH
01/02	09	2 SPANISH I	Y		D	D	0.500	0.500	JFHIGH
01/02	09	2 WRLD HIST I	Y		F	F	0.500	0.000	JFHIGH
01/02	09	ALGEBRA I	Y	F		F	0.500	0.000	JFHIGH
01/02	09	CIVICS	Y	D		D	0.500	0.500	JFHIGH
01/02	09	HEALTH	Y	C		C	0.500	0.500	JFHIGH
01/02	09	HONOR ENG 103	Y	C		C	0.500	0.500	JFHIGH
01/02	09	INT SCIENCE	Y	B		B	0.500	0.500	JFHIGH
01/02	09	MARCHING BAND	Y	B		B	0.500	0.500	JFHIGH
01/02	09	SPANISH I	Y	C		C	0.500	0.500	JFHIGH
						TOTAL	5.750		
02/03	10	1 ALG I	Y	F		F	0.500	0.000	JFHIGH
02/03	10	1 BIOLOGY I	Y	D		D	0.500	0.500	JFHIGH
02/03	10	1 MARCHING BAND	Y	B		B	0.500	0.500	JFHIGH
02/03	10	1 WLD HIST I	Y	D		D	0.500	0.500	JFHIGH
02/03	10	2 BIO I	Y		D	D	0.500	0.500	JFHIGH
02/03	10	2 CONCERT BAND	Y		A	A	0.500	0.500	JFHIGH
02/03	10	2 PARENTING	Y		D	D	0.625	0.625	JFHIGH
02/03	10	2 PHYS ED	Y		B	B	0.250	0.250	JFHIGH
02/03	10	AL I	Y		C	C	0.500	0.500	SU WAYNE
02/03	10	ALGEBRA I	Y		C	C	0.500	0.500	HUBER SS
02/03	10	ENG 201	Y	D		D	0.500	0.500	JFHIGH
02/03	10	ENG 202 2	Y		D	D	0.500	0.500	JFHIGH
02/03	10	SPA II	Y		D	D	0.500	0.500	JFHIGH
02/03	10	SPAN II	Y	D		D	0.500	0.500	JFHIGH
02/03	10	STUDY SKILLS I	Y	B		B	0.500	0.500	JFHIGH
						TOTAL	6.875		
03/04	11	1 ACCOUNTING	Y	B		B	0.500	0.500	JFHIGH
03/04	11	1 US STUDIES	Y	D		D	0.500	0.500	JFHIGH
03/04	11	2 ACCOUNTING	Y		C	C	0.500	0.500	JFHIGH
03/04	11	2 AMERICRN GOV	Y		F	F	0.500	0.000	JFHIGH
03/04	11	CHEMISTRY	Y	F		F	0.500	0.000	JFHIGH
03/04	11	CONCERT BAND	Y	D		D	0.500	0.500	JFHIGH
03/04	11	ENG 301	Y	C		C	0.500	0.500	JFHIGH
03/04	11	ENG 302	Y		F	F	0.500	0.000	JFHIGH
03/04	11	ENG11	Y		B	B	1.000	1.000	LEARN&EVAL
03/04	11	GEOLOGY	Y	F		F	0.500	0.000	JFHIGH
03/04	11	GEOMETRY	Y		F	F	0.500	0.000	JFHIGH
03/04	11	GEOMETRY	Y	F		F	0.500	0.000	JFHIGH
03/04	11	MARCHING BAND	Y	F		F	0.500	0.000	JFHIGH
03/04	11	NUTR & WELLNS	Y	D		D	0.625	0.625	JFHIGH
						TOTAL	4.125		
04/05	12	AMER GOVERNMENT	Y	D	D	D	1.000	1.000	JFHIGH
04/05	12	BUS LAW	Y	A	D	D	1.000	1.000	JFHIGH
04/05	12	ENGL 12	Y		C	C	1.000	1.000	LEARN&EVAL
04/05	12	ENGLISH 12	Y	D	F	F	1.000	0.000	JFHIGH
04/05	12	ERTHSCI1	Y		A	A	1.000	1.000	LEARN&EVAL
04/05	12	GEOMETRY	Y	D	D	D	1.000	1.000	JFHIGH
04/05	12	INT MATH I	Y	C	D	D	1.000	1.000	JFHIGH

OHIO PROFICIENCY SCORES:

	DATE	SCORE	SCALED

ACT SCORES:

TEST DATE	/	/	/	/
ENGLISH				
MATH				
READING				
SCI REAS				
COMPOSITE				
ENG/WRITING				
WRITING				

SAT SCORES:

TEST DATE	GRADE	SAT VERBAL	SAT MATH
/			
/			

My high school transcript

At my high school they pretty much passed everybody, so to fail a class you had to do below absolutely nothing, meaning you had to either skip school habitually, plus disrespect the learning process when you were present, and I checked both of those boxes. I failed Geometry my junior year and was forced to repeat it as a last hooray during my senior year, where I barely passed with a D. Senior year my Geometry teacher was a tall middle-aged black man from DeSoto Bass housing projects, Dr. Richard Gates. Dr. Gates was one of the only black teachers that I had during high school, and he always preached the importance of being solid in math and performing well on the ACT. I truly appreciated him passing me along, when my back was completely against the wall. The graduation requirements for math in Ohio during that time required that you passed Geometry. As you can see from my high school transcript, I was certainly a low-performing, at-risk student to say the least. I count a total of 63 D's and F's on my high school transcript, and I definitely earned more than that. For me graduating high school and surviving my environment was a feat within itself, and I was in no way prepared for the years that followed.

"I used to act up when I went to school, thought it was cool, but I really

was hurt"

Meek Mill - Oodles O' Noodles Babies

CHAPTER III
Fight or Flight

What I learned later in life from reading books like *Helping Children Succeed* by Paul Tough, is that my executive functions had been profoundly impacted due to my adverse environmental conditions. Executive functions impact an individual's cognitive flexibility, working memory, and inhibitory control. Here is a list of skills impacted by executive functions.

- Paying attention
- Organizing, planning and prioritizing
- Starting tasks and staying focused on them to completion
- Understanding different points of view
- Regulating emotions
- Self-monitoring (keeping track of what you're doing)

Last year I learned about the Adverse Childhood Experience study (ACEs) from a TED Talk by Dr. Nadine Harris. I will try to describe my takeaways from her brilliant speech. During the speech Dr. Harris explained how she was exposed to the ACEs study, which was conducted by Vincent J. Felitti M.D, and Bob Anda M.D. ACEs is a study that researched exposure to adverse childhood experiences, and the long-term impacts of these experiences. Dr. Felitti and Dr. Anda interviewed 17,500 adults asking them questions regarding specific adverse experiences. Below are some of the questions listed on the ACEs study, for every yes to a question, the participant would receive one point on their ACEs score.

- Sexual abuse
- Emotional abuse
- Physical abuse
- Physical neglect
- Emotional neglect

- Intimate partner violence
- Mother treated violently
- Substance misuse within household
- Household mental illness
- Parental separation or divorce
- Incarcerated household member

The researchers then correlated the ACEs scores against long-term health outcomes and concluded that a higher ACEs score led to worse individual's health outcomes. Some critics of the study argued that this was not a groundbreaking discovery, as individuals with difficult childhoods are more likely to engage in high-risk behavior (smoking, alcohol abuse, drugs, etc.). But the study revealed that regardless of participation in high-risk behavior, individuals with higher ACEs scores are 3x more likely to develop heart disease and cancer. **The higher your ACEs score, the worse your health outcomes.** This is because repeated stress activation among children negatively impacts brain structure, brain development and function, the developing immune system, developing hormonal system, and the way DNA is read and transcribed. Children are especially sensitive to the repeated activation of the stress response because their brains and bodies are just developing. High doses of adversity in childhood actually shapes the way the brain develops, also known as brain architecture. This process is byproduct of the Hypothalamic–pituitary–adrenal axis, the brain and body's stress response system, also known as **Fight or Flight**.

Childhood trauma - threats that are so severe or pervasive that they literally get under our skin and change our physiology.

"Children are especially sensitive to this repeated stress activation

because their brains and bodies are just developing."

Dr. Nadine Harris

Here is how the Fight or Flight system works.

1.   Your hypothalamus sends a signal to your pituitary
2.   Pituitary sends the signal to your adrenal gland
3.   This signal is interpreted by the adrenal and tells your body to release stress hormones, adrenaline and cortisol

This Fight or Flight system is a crucial component of adaptation and survival. If we suddenly encounter a bear in the wilderness, our brains would innately activate the Fight or Flight system, which helps prepare the body to either fight the bear or run from it. For children growing up in stressful environments, Fight or Flight becomes counterproductive due to repeated activation, which negatively impacts long-term health outcomes. Every night when a rat would scurry across me while I slept on the floor, or every time Grandma smashed a roach with her flat, I was activating my stress response system. When I flashback to my childhood, I am instantly overcome by those childhood fears. I envision rats running amuck through the kitchen, roaches crawling up and down the walls, inside the microwave, and across the gas stove. I feel the discomfort and anxiety from sleeping on the floor. I wish that I could replace those memories with trips to the zoo or family vacations. Although both are memories, only the former leaves scars. Even today my sensitivity towards rodents is extremely high, I cannot sit in a room or house that has any type of rodent problem. I remember hearing scratches in the wall at my Aunt's house a few years ago due to a squirrel or raccoon that had broken in through the chimney. During my stay I was unable to concentrate on anything else but the scratching noise and my fear of the animal. I refused to use the bathroom, and ultimately had to cut my trip short. A major study on ACEs was done by Kaiser and the Center for Disease Control and Prevention (CDC), those people who were exposed to six or more ACEs had a twenty-year difference in life expectancy. The trauma from my childhood experience will take a lifetime to cope. I calculated my ACEs total score as an eight.

"Childhood trauma isn't something you just get over as you grow up"

Dr. Nadine Harris

CHAPTER IV
Toledo, Ohio

"We used to be like distant cousins, fightin', playin' dozens

Whole neighborhood buzzin', knowin', that we wasn't"

Tupac Shakur

In 2007 Grannie Payne sold her 1998 Buick Lesabre to me for $200 bucks which was an absolute steal, the same one my dad had slammed me on seven or so years earlier. Everybody knows how good older people take care of their cars, especially older black church ladies and their beloved Buicks. The Buick had leather seats, power windows, a cd player, and a brown soft-top. After sitting out from college during the Fall 2006, I decided I needed to transfer to an in-state school, somewhere cheaper that would allow me to use more state based financial aid. A few of my homies were at the University of Toledo, and after listening to their persuasive pitches about the girls and the campus Rec center, I decided that I'd apply as a transfer student, but made no formal commitment. The University of Toledo (UT) had an open enrollment admission policy, so as long as you graduated from an Ohio public school you could be granted admission. This was obviously a crucial factor in my decision, because I'm doubtful that I would have been accepted by another University based on my lack of academic success.

Torrey was also trying to figure out his next move in life, and that autumn we did a whole lot of nothing together. I remember walking up to his Dad's house almost every day to play Madden for hours on end. If I wasn't at work, I was over Torrey's, anything to stay out of Grandma's house. We would steal his dads spare change that he kept in a large clear jar in his room, and use it to order pizza, then go back in his room for more change, and walk to the corner store for a gallon of chilly-willy juice. Torrey was determined to play college football, and I knew that I had enough game to walk on to a college basketball squad. So together we decided we would go to UT and try our hand at walking on for our respective sports. There was about ten or so guys I was cool with from Dayton who attended UT, and together we got into all kinds of trouble. My cousin Bear, my cousin Nick, my cousin Nate, Ced, Marvell, Donye, and Cam. Nate was on the Football Team at UT, and although he was younger, he definitely was the most disciplined of the crew. Together we dined and dashed from local restaurants, stole clothes from the mall, partied, drank, played basketball for hours on end, and most of all, skipped class. Toledo was an interesting time, I was surrounded by genuine love from guys I had known for a while, and we were all out of the house, and experiencing this thing called college together.

Torrey, me, and some random cats from UT

Officer Kline - Ohio State Patrol

The best part about Toledo was that I was much closer to Dayton in comparison to WKU. At WKU I caught the Greyhound back to Dayton often to visit my girlfriend at the time, but at Toledo I could easily drive or catch a ride back to the city to hang out with childhood friends and the like. This was the plan one chilly Friday evening when I departed from Toledo heading back to Dayton. On March 30, 2007 I was driving southbound on I-75 with my homeboy Donye. I was cruising at about 70 MPH when Donye said, "Do this mug go any faster." Feeling slightly disrespected by his comment I hit the gas and turned up a new Lil Wayne mixtape that I had burned exclusively for the trip. I had got the Buick up to about 84 MPH and no less than two minutes later I saw a patrol car pull out as I sped by, my heart sank to my stomach. The highway patrolman caught up with us and I immediately pulled over to the side of the highway. The officer rushed to Donye's side, "License and registration", I explained to the officer that I knew my license ID number but couldn't find my actual license. "So you don't have a license, get out of the car." I got out and the officer shoved me against the side of the Buick, patted me down and asked, "You got any drugs on ya," "No sir, I am a college student," I responded. He advised me to stay put while he returned to his squad car to run my information. He emerged ten minutes later and said, "Looks like your license is suspended due to an SR22," I knew that was a possibility because I was late paying my car insurance. I was required to keep an SR22 on file with GEICO due to the first ticket I received while delivering pizzas for Papa John's. He proceeded to handcuff me, "You can either pay $300, or I'm taking you to jail." I called Aunt Cynthia first, she said she didn't have $300 and hung up abruptly. Then I called my Dad, who echoed those sentiments. I would have called Granny Payne first, but I didn't want to wake her, but as I was dialing her number Officer Kline snatched my T-Mobile Dash, "That's enough calls." By this time two more squad cars had pulled up, a different officer asked if he could search the vehicle and I conceded knowing that I had nothing to hide. All I had in the trunk was my golf clubs and some jars of vanilla protein. I remember the second officer opening my Vanilla Whey

Protein and running his finger through to ensure it wasn't powdered cocaine. Officer Kline tightened my handcuffs and told me to get in the squad car. "These are too tight," I exclaimed, "Keep squirming they get tighter." As I was walking to the squad car Donye emerged and said, "Aye Sho can I take this Weezy mix," I just shook my head as to say, "Nigga are you serious." Officer Kline called in a tow for my vehicle, and another officer gave Donye a ride to the closest Denny's. I was handcuffed in the backseat and Officer Kline pulled from the shoulder headed southbound towards Dayton, presumably taking me to the closest jail to the city. A call came through on his radio, "Where's he from", the dispatcher asked, "I think the boy is from Dayton," Kline responded. "Well don't take him towards Dayton make it hard on his ass, take him to Hitchcock County," the dispatcher responded. Officer Kline abruptly turned the squad car around in the median and started traveling back towards Toledo, and further away from my hometown and original destination. At this point I was fighting back tears asking the officer why he was taking me to this random jail and why couldn't I call my Grandmother. "Shut up, we're almost there, and you better be careful at Hitchcock," Kline said with a malicious undertone. He pulled into the jail, opened my door, finally loosened the cuffs, and walked me inside. I was booked and placed in a holding cell all night. That morning I saw a Judge, hands and feet shackled, wearing the same outfit I had been in for over 24 hours. The Judge asked me what law I had broken, and I explained, "Sir, I am a college student at the University of Toledo, I was arrested for speeding and driving under a suspended license due not being able to afford my insurance this month." "Why would he take you to jail for that, and you say you're in college," he responded. "Yes sir," I said confidently, he then asked for my plea to the charges. I was unclear on how to plea, and I had never stood in front of a judge or been handcuffed, "No contest sir," I said with a crackling voice. A couple people in the courtroom began laughing and someone said, "Dumbass now you have to come back to court." They were right. I would have to come back to Findlay, Ohio for court due to my ignorance of the judicial system and not making a firm plea.

Three weeks later I returned to court and stood in front of a totally different magistrate, Judge Robert Fry. Prior to my appearance I watched Judge Fry hand out extremely light sentences to several white people for what I considered to be far worse than driving with a suspended license. No jail time, no community service, some didn't even get their licenses suspended. I remember one white guy was cited for drunk driving that caused an accident, which resulted in the victim being paralyzed, Judge Fry gave no jail time and said, "I think living with what you did is punishment enough." By the time I stood before the podium wearing an oversized navy-blue suit, Judge Fry seemed to be all out of cutting breaks. I was sentenced to thirty days in jail for driving with a suspended license, the maximum sentence for the crime. I couldn't believe it, for only my second ticket in life! After a long pause the Judge said, "All of which will be suspended with the defendant completing 50 hours of community service." I had been given a deadline of July 9, 2007. I was still stunned, by what seemed to be a drastic over sentence, especially based on all of the previous slaps on the wrist I heard that morning. I knew I needed to work full-time during the summer so finding time to complete 50 hours of community service was going to be cumbersome to say the least.

PWI: *Predominantly White Institution*

SES: *Socio-economic status*

ShoMari Payne

KEVIN C SMITH, Judge
ROBERT A FRY, Judge
MARSHA OKULY, Clerk
DAVID D BEACH,
Director of Court Services

Findlay Municipal Court
Municipal Building
Findlay, Ohio 45840
Telephone 419-424-7141
Fax 419-424-7803

COMMITMENT PENDING HEARING

Case Number: 07TRD02267 A

FINDLAY MUNICIPAL COURT

2007 MAR 30 A 10 57

State of Ohio vs **SHOMARI N PAYNE**

DOB: 09/22/1987

Bail set at $300.00   **10% Allowed Yes / No**

To the Hancock County Justice Center;

Whereas, SHOMARI N PAYNE has been arrested on the oath of Officer KLINE, TYLER of State Patrol for 4510.16A DUS - FRA, NONCOMPLIANCE
4511.21D2 SPEED-USE ONLY FOR 65 MPH ZONE and has been brought before said Court and has been postponed until: **April 10, 2007 at 01:15 PM.**

Therefore, in the name of the State of Ohio, you are commanded to receive the said defendant into your custody, in the jail of the county aforesaid, there to remain until discharged by due course of law.

Witness my signature and the seal of said court, on March 30, 2007.

MARSHA OKULY
Clerk

Deputy Clerk

KEVIN C SMITH, Judge
ROBERT A FRY, Judge
MARSHA OKULY, Clerk
DAVID D BEACH,
Director of Court Services

Findlay Municipal Court
Municipal Building
Findlay, Ohio 45840
Telephone 419-424-7141
Fax 419-424-7903

SUPERVISED COMMUNITY SERVICE PROGRAM
FINDLAY MUNICIPAL COURT

Case Number: 07TRD02267

Name:	SHOMARI N PAYNE	Judge: ROBERT A FRY
Address:	1550 KIMMEL LN	Sentencing Date: 04/10/2007
	DAYTON, OH 45418	To perform 50 Hours service
County:	MONTOMGERY	to be completed by 07/09/2007
Phone:	937-878-2008	

WAIVER AND RELEASE

The undersigned __SHOMARI N PAYNE__ , in the above numbered case in the Municipal Court of Findlay, Ohio, on behalf of myself, my heirs, executors, administrators, and assigns, in consideration of placement and acceptance into the Supervised Community Service Program, hereby:

1. Agree to faithfully perform and complete the Community Service Program as a condition of my sentence as directed by the supervisor of the assigned agency.

2. Agree that I am not an employee of the assigned Community Service Agency or the Findlay Municipal Court at any time during my participation and performance in the program and am not entitled to any employee benefits, rights or protection; I agree to pay a $25.00 administration fee; I agree to report for registration within 7 calendar days of conviction.

3. I acknowledge that if I fail to preform my community service satisfactorily within the time specified a BENCH WARRANT will be issued for my arrest and I will serve my sentence in the Hancock County Justice Center. I understand it is my responsibility to report to any restrictions on my activities or health problems to the agency supervisor. I will not consume alcohol or drugs prior to or during the performance of community service. I will present identification upon registration for service.

4. I agree to waive, discharge, release and hold harmless the City of Finday, the Findlay Municipal Court, Hancock County, and any and all others employed by them from every claim, liability, demand, action or cause of action of any kind or for on account of any personal injury or any other form of damage to person or property sustained by me or caused by me while participating or performing in the Supervised Community Service Program, and voluntarily assume all risk of accident or damage to my person or property.

103

My college career at the University of Toledo began during the Spring 2007 semester, and I was academically dismissed from the institution at the end of the semester. Bear, Torrey, Nick, and Nate were my main homies in Toledo, and I was devastated that I wouldn't be returning back to the University with them. Many other cats from Dayton started as UT students, but slowly transitioned to strictly Toledo locals. I didn't love Toledo enough to live there and not be enrolled in the University, so I knew I wasn't going back. I had earned 3 F's, and two Withdrawals during my lone semester at UT. My next pressing question was where I would be sleeping that summer, I refused to go back to Grandma Clark's house, I never wanted to step foot in that place again. I promised myself that I'd sleep on the garage floor in another relative's house before I'd ever stay there. After Grannie Payne sold the house she moved back to her hometown of Richmond, Virginia. Richmond was always Grandpa and Grannie Payne's true home, and she wanted to be closer to her siblings and family. That summer I took the only job offer that came my way, third shift at a Speedway in Huber Heights, Ohio. I stayed with Aunt Cynthia and Ali which was ironic because Aunt Cynthia was the first person I called to avoid all of the calamity I went through in Findlay. She definitely was not hurting for $300, but I am not her son or her responsibility, so I couldn't fault her for not bailing me out. I just always thought Ali and I were a package deal, and I know she would have never let Ali go to jail for such a small amount of change or any amount for that matter. But despite working full time at Speedway, I avoided my thirty days in jail by completing my community service at a DHL warehouse in East Dayton, just in the nick of time.

CHAPTER V
Return to the Bluegrass

I originally started college at Western Kentucky University in the Fall of 2005 at seventeen years old, and by the Spring 2007 I had finished my second year of being a college student, but as far as credit hours, I was still a freshman. In two years of college I managed to accumulate just 12 credit hours and a 1.59 GPA. A failed stint at WKU and UT had me wondering if I had the discipline, knowledge, financial capital, or academic skills to succeed in college. That summer Ali's Grandpa on his mom's side passed away. Although he wasn't biologically my Grandfather, he was an elder that I truly respected, and he always treated me with love during our few encounters. I called him Grandpa Flemming just as Ali did, and I certainly was going to pay my respects. Uncle Barry drove Ali and I down to the funeral in Columbia, South Carolina. While driving through the Kentucky mountains I couldn't help but reminisce about WKU. There was something nostalgic about WKU, it was the first place I called home after my seventeen years of bondage. During that drive all those old feelings I felt about WKU resurfaced, it was like falling in love all over again. I thought about those fulfilling meals at the campus sports bar, I began revisioning the campus architecture and my connection to it. I started thinking about those intense lifting sessions at the Rec center, some of the pretty southern girls I had dated. During this daydream something dawned on me. I remembered that I was never technically kicked out of WKU (as was the case with UT), I was just short on tuition money. It was on that drive through the Bluegrass mountains that I made the decision to return back to Western Kentucky University, a place where I hadn't had any academic success, but to me was home.

As soon as we returned to Ohio I slapped a for sale sign on the Buick so that I could pay my outstanding balance and return to WKU. The Lesabre was definitely worth at least $2,500, but I took the first offer that came my way and settled for $1,000. I told myself that this go around I would take college serious, and put forth my best effort, and selling the Buick was my way of having some real skin in the game. I returned to WKU during the Fall 2007, but I never lived in Bowling Green, Kentucky without transportation, and without a car it was impossible for me to find work. I applied for campus jobs, but never heard back (probably due to my atrocious GPA). Although I was more focused, I still faced many barriers that impacted my ability to be even an average college student. I was always hungry, and soon learned that I could not afford to charge a meal plan to my account and also cover tuition with financial aid, so I opted out of the meal plan. Growing up I always ate for free at school because our household income qualified me for the Free and Reduced Lunch program. But in college you are not obligated to a free meal, and those of us whose student ID's were without sufficient balances were often viewed as second class citizens. I remember hovering around the Fresh Food buffet on campus hoping I could slip by the student workers to gain access to the all you can eat smorgasbord. When that plan was foiled I would try to bum some meal swipes from friends, but that grows old for both parties after the second or third ask. So here I was back in Kentucky, encountering some friendly faces from freshman year, but many unfamiliar ones. I got real cool with a dude from Paducah, Kentucky named Lamar Alston. Lamar was a former defensive back at the University of Louisville, he was kicked off the team for failing too many drug tests. Lamar transferred to WKU in the Fall of 2007, and I could relate to where he was at life, a young man searching for a second chance. Lamar and I worked out together daily at Preston (Campus Rec center), my goal was to help him walk-on to the football team at WKU, and to develop my skills as a personal trainer. But as the old adage says, "Old habits die hard," and it proved to be a tall order keeping Lamar away from the ganja. This was the first time in my life that I had smoked weed, and although I wasn't really a fan, it was a central aspect of our friendship. We would smoke a blunt then hit up this local Mexican restaurant called Pepper's, or smoke in the campus parking lot called Egypt and listen to UGK in his jet-black Chevy Caprice that he swore was a 96' Impala SS. I didn't smoke as much as Lamar did, but we smoked enough to offset the goals I had set for myself at the beginning of the semester. Lamar ultimately walked on to the team no problem, his credentials spoke for themselves and we trained pretty hard. But for me, I had tricked off another year of school, and was faced with the recurring question, where was I going to stay this summer.

Lamar and me outside our dorm, Pearce Ford Tower - WKU

CHAPTER VI
Summer 2008

Kroger Parking Lot - Canal Winchester, Ohio

For the Summer of 2008 I landed on Columbus, Ohio as my host city. I remember pleading with Dad to allow me to stay with him, hoping that I could find better work in the State Capitol than I did the summer prior at Speedway in the Dayton area. I was partly right because after only a few days in Columbus I landed a gig as a sales associate at TNT Fashions on E. Broad Street (my second stint with the company), and another as a sales associate in the hardware department at Walmart on E.Main Street. Both jobs were in close proximity to the DSCC base, so I rode to work with Dad every morning. Dad would drop me off at the base gym around 5:00 am, I'd workout until it was time to shower and prepare for my first shift at TNT. I'd walk to TNT Fashions for a 6-hour shift, then walk three miles to Walmart and work until the store closed. In total I was bringing in about $600/week and would soon reach my goal of buying a 2001 Chevrolet Impala before school started back.

Two Eggs Later

It was a normal July morning for me, I woke up at my Dad's apartment and decided to scramble myself two eggs before hitching a ride with him for a daily work ritual. He came downstairs and didn't say much, but upon opening the refrigerator he realized that I had taken the last two eggs. "ShoMari, how many eggs did you cook", I responded, "Just two Pops", "Got damnit boy don't you know we are in a recession, you eat one egg in this house. I'm taking you to the store when you get off and you buying your own damn eggs." I didn't have a problem with that, and figured he'd lose his attitude by the time he picked me up from work. After my shift, I hopped in his blue Chevy Trailblazer and attempted to tell him about my day, but he indeed managed to carry his attitude, so I shut up and put my headphones on. We arrived at Kroger and he said, "Don't be taking all day, you know Karma is dropping Camille off at 6:30," I responded, "No problem Pop," and we dispersed throughout the store. We had about 30 minutes before my sister (his youngest daughter) was getting dropped off by her mom (Karma), so I grabbed some Gatorade, eggs, bread, and headed to checkout. Dad was first in line, then a lady with a decent number of items in her cart, then me. After Dad checked out, he came and investigated my few items, "That's all you getting, don't be complaining later that you hungry and don't be eating up all my shit." I realized he was trying to pick a fight, so I just completely ignored him. Thirty seconds later he approached me again, "And you get behind this lady with all this shit in her cart, you ain't about to have Karma cussing me out." At this point onlookers in the store seemed concerned, some were laughing, but many were just standing by witnessing a man have a public breakdown. Due to the embarrassment I opted to leave my items and said, "It's cool let's just go, don't want us to be late," and walked past him heading back towards the car. He darted after me, blocked my path, and stood directly in my face, "No go back and get your shit, ain't tryna here your mouth later either." I asked him in a calm voice to get out of my face, he responded, "What you gonna do," I gave him a light shove and he stumbled back dramatically as if he was in danger of falling, it was an Oscar performance, I barely touched him. He returned to my face, "You gon put your hands on me, I never put my hands on my Dad, you ain't no son of mine, fuck ya, fuck ya, ya shit will be outside." He marched towards his Chevy trailblazer, opened the back hatch, threw my golf clubs on the ground behind him, reversed over them like an old speed bump, and gave me one last "fuck ya" while flipping me the bird before he skirted off. Immediately following the ordeal an older black woman walked up to me and said, "You didn't do anything wrong baby, I saw the whole thing, I am so sorry that's your Dad." I gave the woman a hug and said thank you. I went up to the parking spot, picked up my golf clubs, and started walking back towards his apartment. I knew my dad was nuts when he slammed me on Grannie Payne's Buick, but this was an even lower move in my opinion. I picked up the game of golf in an attempt to spend more time with him since he loved the game. I figured if we had something in common it would give us something to bond over, a reason for him to want to spend some time with me. I found it extremely unnecessary for him to go out of his way to pitch my golf clubs onto the pavement, and then run them over. To me that was symbolic of him saying no matter how hard I tried to cultivate a relationship, he wanted nothing to do with me.

I had a solid four mile walk beneath the blistering July sun to get to his apartment from Kroger, but I was built for it due to my summer workout regimen. When I arrived at his apartment the time was precisely 7:15 pm, Karma was just now arriving with my little sister, which I found amusing since beating her home was the basis for his rage. She pulled up to me in her car, "What happened son," I explained, "This nigga crazy, he cussed me out and left me at Kroger." Karma took me to her house to stay for a few days so things could cool off. This was the second time I had seen so much anger from my dad, and it was completely unprovoked. It gave me a deeper understanding of his views towards me specifically. I was the bastard child, his other two marriages were with women he truly loved, and the children from those marriages were cultivated with love. He had mortgages with those women, family portraits, and happy memories. But he saw something else when he looked at me, and I always felt it, but once Grandpa passed away he had no reason to fake it anymore. That day helped close a chapter in my life that I had left open for far too long. His actions let me know that I needed to stop trying to force myself into his life, and his words became the fuel I needed to push myself through college.

"No, you know what, Uncle Phil? I'ma get through college without him, I'ma get a great job without him, I'ma marry me a beautiful honey, and I'ma have me a whole bunch of kids. I'll be a better father than he ever was, and I sure as hell don't need him for that, 'cause ain't a damn thing he could ever teach me about how to love my kids"
Will Smith - Fresh Prince of Bel'Air

CHAPTER VII
Cap & Gown

"But you know business majors you can't even get a job when you coming up right outta school"
Big Sean

Spending the 2008 summer with Dad had truly lit a fire, I was determined to prove to myself that I was more than the kid that nobody wanted, more than the boy who grew up poor and dusty, more than the near high school dropout, and more than a three-year college freshman, but I had dug myself into a serious hole. I was three years into my college career, but four years of credit hours away from graduating. I was determined not to become another statistic, so I buckled down and formulated a game plan. I still remember that day sitting in my apartment in Bowling Green, Kentucky when I called my Academic

110

Advisor Patricia Jordan. "So, if I take this class, then this class," she cut me off, "Honey I am looking at your transcript, are you sure that college is for you?" I chuckled and said, "Ma'am if you knew my story you would know college is the least of my obstacles." Something about the way I answered must have convinced her that I was seriously committed, and she helped me map out a plan in which I could accelerate my goal of graduation. It wasn't easy, but I unlocked a new level within myself, and became absolutely obsessed with school. I studied in the library, at my apartment, at friends' apartments, and I kept all of my books with me at all times. I brought flashcards with me to work at Cracker Barrel, and spent my lunch breaks quizzing myself on fuzzy topics. I raised my GPA, joined two fraternities (one social, one professional), and managed to balance my part-time job at Cracker Barrel. I only worked on the weekends, two 12 hour shifts back to back, usually a 5:00AM - 5:00PM or 6:00AM to 6:00PM. Despite working only two days a week I managed to wear out the tread on my company issued slip resistant all-black work shoes. This was my schedule for two years straight, and it paid off.

"Low SES students may not have cars, bus fare, or a back-up plan if their transportation system is disrupted"

NPR Higher Ed.

In my community, black excellence is captured after you upload your first college graduation picture on Facebook. In that sense I had captured it, I managed to navigate my way through college in a total of five years, even after completely squandering the first three years. For my final two years at WKU I registered for classes at two colleges simultaneously in an effort to graduate within a "decent" amount of time. This was a tall order for a guy who was literally sitting at the brink of academic dismissal and hadn't accomplished anything that suggested I could pull this off. While taking a full 18 credit hour load at WKU, I also enrolled at Sinclair Community College which was back home in Dayton. At Sinclair I registered for as many classes that would transfer back to WKU. I registered for English, Psychology, Humanities, Biology, Spanish, Economics, and many other general-education courses online at Sinclair in addition to taking my five or six business classes at WKU. I never crafted out a post-college plan, in part because I never really wanted to leave college. Working at Miami University today has provided me with a crucial understanding of how wealthy families map out their children's futures long before they are even born. My background lacked wealth and support, but I was determined to at least walk across that stage. And on Dec. 18, 2010 I accomplished that goal, exactly six years after I lost my Grandpa.

Graduation day - Dec. 18, 2010

Higher Education

"Attending Miami was my short-term goal during my high school life. I heard of the Farmer School of Business a lot from both my teachers and friends"

Sarah Wang - International Student

"Higher educated parents help provide greater opportunities like summer STEM camps, musical instruments, and trips to Europe"

Dr. Janice Kinghorn - Professor of Economics Miami University

At the time of this writing I work as an educator at Miami University. Miami University is located in Oxford, Ohio, and is one of the oldest public universities in the country, made possible by an ordinance signed by President George Washington in 1795. Chartered in 1809, Miami welcomed its first students in 1824. Miami's reputation grew as quickly as its enrollment, and it became known as the "Yale of the West" for its ambitious liberal arts curriculum. Today, Miami consistently ranks among the nation's top public universities for the quality of teaching and overall student experience. Miami University is nicknamed, "The Public Ivy", and I have been fortunate enough to advise, teach, and mentor some of the brightest young minds in the country while working in the Farmer School of Business. Many of my students explained to me that attending Miami was a foregone conclusion because their parents are both Miami Alumni, otherwise known as "Miami mergers." I have built lifelong relationships with students from across the globe, students that hail from prestigious international high schools like the Hanoi School for the Gifted in Vietnam, Beijing Normal University, and Chongqing No.8 Secondary School. A large percentage of Miami student's hail from what we refer to as the four C's, Cincinnati, Columbus, Cleveland, and Chicago. Many students from the four C's attended elite private high schools such as Lake Forest Academy in Chicago, Illinois, Saint

Xavier in Cincinnati, Ohio, Saint Charles in Columbus, Ohio, and Saint Ignatius in Cleveland, Ohio.

The Farmer School of Business has been ranked as the No. 17 public business school in the country by Poets & Quants magazine in its 2018 *Top Undergraduate Business Schools* in the nation, and the top business school in Ohio. Students in the Farmer School of Business are positioned for fortune 500 internships, followed by very competitive job offers. They are privy to executive speaker presentations from industry experts, illustrious study abroad opportunities, and are connected to a vast network of successful alumni in various high-level positions throughout the business world. Miami University is approximately 45 minutes from my high school, but I legitimately had never heard of it. The colleges that I had heard of where due to the big games on Saturday mornings, schools like Ohio State and Michigan, schools like Sinclair Community College and the University of Dayton as a result of grade school field trips. Neither of my parents found it necessary to discuss my future plans, not once, maybe because they were both were too concerned with their own lives.

Looking back, I never stood a chance of attaining my "dream job" after college, not based on the minimal information I held, and the lack of resources I possessed. My social capital was completely nonexistent. I wasn't aware that families had dinner table conversations about college, weighing pros and cons, discussing tuition costs, researching accomplished alumni, reviewing program offerings, comparing job-placement rates, exploring co-op/internship data, and most importantly discussing the impact of family legacy. I never had the experience of my future holding so much weight in the eyes of my parents and made no such considerations before deciding on WKU. Nevertheless, the day I graduated from college, I figured that soon I would be writing my own ticket. I assumed my subpar Microsoft excel skills combined with an above-par personality would land me my first corporate gig at Nike or the NBA shortly after graduation. Eventually reality set in that I was in no position to land a position as a sports agent, or a marketing gig working for Nike, no matter how confident I was, or how many campus speaker presentations I had attended. I remember my senior year of undergrad, a former Director of Marketing for the NBA, Dan Opallo, visited campus and spoke to the business students. I recorded his speech and memorized it, believing that when Nike or the NBA called me up on my application, I would impress them with my extensive marketing knowledge and professional business acumen. At the end of Dan's presentation, he gave out his number (as they all do) and encouraged us to give him a call if we were ever in the NYC area. He promised he would score us some Knicks tickets and a nice dinner. Although I've never been to NYC, I texted him multiple times hoping for a reference, but as expected I never got a response, not even sure that was his real number. That's how a young black boy from the inner city thought the world worked, I was assured that I was owed some cosmic justice for how I was raised, and I was confident it would come in the form of a six-figure job that required a suit, minimal work, lots of handshakes, and plenty of international travel. I was unable to secure any serious job offers upon graduating from college. I didn't know then, but my degree and GPA carried minimal weight in an economy still recovering from the Great Recession. Recruiters were not scouring my campus looking for their next marketing analyst, or corporate tax accountant. Majority of my college cohort returned home and started working in the same positions we could have garnered without our $50,000 piece of paper. Call center representatives, servers at restaurants, sales associates, or the occasional entry level sales rep at Enterprise or Hertz. Many of us were confined to what the business industry calls "Gray-Collar" positions.

Dan Opallo - Former NBA Director of Marketing

Rude Awakening

My first job out of college was working as a teller for U.S Bank in Bowling Green, Kentucky. This job provided me with my first case of workplace discrimination. As the only black employee at the large main branch I found it pretty difficult to adjust, but I found a niche in just keeping my mouth shut and focusing on the customers. One night the entire team was required to stay late so that we could brainstorm ideas on how to get more foot traffic into the branch. A few of the ladies from the finance team threw out some ideas such as a cowboy themed day or wear your favorite team jersey. But then one lady made a comment that seemed harmless at first, "Or we can be like P-Diddy and throw a white-out party, well except for ShoMari, we'll just cover him up with an ole white sheet." The entire team broke out into hysteria, but I just sat there with a stone-cold look. There was one more person in the room who wasn't laughing, and that was my manager, Brian Woods. Brian sent me a text before the meeting was over that read, "I do not approve of that comment, we will discuss first thing tomorrow." This was the first time that I felt ostracized by a room full of white people. Most African-Americans associate white sheets with the Ku Klux Klan, and being the only black employee at a bank in Bowling Green, Kentucky didn't help alleviate that natural affinity. For the next several weeks I was treated to carry-in lunches from upscale restaurants, treated to BW3's for lunch with Brian, and received overall peculiar treatment. This ordeal culminated in a top floor meeting with the regional president Craig Browning. I had seen Craig a few times in passing, but we had never said more than hi and bye. This day in his top floor suite Craig asked me a series of questions regarding my next steps regarding the comment. "Do you plan on getting any outside organizations involved," he asked. I told him that I was over it, and I didn't want the lady to get in any trouble, "She feels terrible, it was an honest mistake," Craig reiterated. But after this incident I knew that I needed to work around more people who looked like me, or at least we're a little more sensitive to race. I didn't really know where to go, or who would hire a marketing major that graduated with a 2.3 from a subpar business school, and whose sole internship was at the campus Rec Center. But after some careful thought I decided I'd go back to the same place I never really wanted to leave, back into education.

2010 Internship at the Preston Rec Center

I knew that I could use my new degree to make $13/hour as a substitute teacher, which was $4 more than I made as a part-time teller at U.S Bank, and $5 more than I made as a 2-star host at Cracker Barrel. So I obtained a background check and took my talents to the same school systems that played a part in my disconnection from the economic realities of the age. The first time I subbed, I was mesmerized by the chaos and lack of institutional control. I fell into the familiar rhetoric that most old school black elders use when referring to kids these days, "We wasn't that bad," or, "They need to bring paddling back," and the old trusty, "Too many kids having kids." My last two years at WKU had groomed a level of normality into my demeanor. I began to appreciate the arts, jazz music, trips to the museum, an occasional steak dinner, community service, reading books, and a quiet study day at the library. This level of maturity, cultural appreciation, and calmness had not been present during my upbringing, this was brought about from college, and the separation from my childhood environment.

But as a brand-new educator I was thinking from a place of ignorance. I was not recalling the historical ingredients that led to such chaos. I had not yet been educated on the discriminatory housing policies of the New Deal, and the segregation that permeated. I had not yet learned about how the decline of the manufacturing industry, the Federal highway act, suburbanization, white flight, public housing projects, and how the lack of city taxes had decimated the public-school systems of major cities. I had not read the New Jim Crow, and learned of the discrepancy in sentencing between crack and cocaine, the system of mass incarceration, or the private prison industry. I was not educated on the cognitive impacts of growing up in stressful environments, dilapidated homes, sleeping amiss loud noise, malnourishment, and the detrimental impacts of growing up without someone reading to you during developing years. I had some understanding of the role poverty and absent parents played in my own ignorance, development, and lack of opportunity, but I had never tied it back to a fully functioning system.

"I dedicate these words to you and all the other children affected by the

mass incarceration of this nation, that sent ya pops to prison when he

needed education"

J.Cole - 4 Your Eyez Only

CHAPTER VIII
I Need Security

"Y'all don't even check our book-bags"
Dayton Public School Student

"Cuz it ain't nothin in em, I been doing this 20 years"
Security guard, Dayton Public Schools

May 6, 2016

Teaching in the inner-city was a tall-order, but an experience I will always cherish. During the 2015-2016 school year I taught full-time as a PE Teacher for World of Wonder PK-8(WOW), in the Dayton Public School district. After work I'd arrive to my townhome in Huber Heights, Ohio, sink into the belly of my cheap leather couch, and lay there for hours. I was physically exhausted from breaking up fights, and mentally drained from the obscene rhetoric I heard from kids on a daily basis, each day was a battle onto itself. I remember once a 3rd grade girl intentionally launched a fully inflated basketball at my private area, if I was a weaker man I would have been floored. I called her parents to inform them of the incident and her father proceeded to cuss me smooth out, "Should of been wearing a cup, punk ass nigga," he said in response to my explanation of the occurrence. But one day in particular stands out above the rest. It was a normal school day, as our scrawny security guard Bryant would often say, "It's quiet on the front." He really was pretty scrawny, one time a rambunctious 6th grader named Jabril called Mr. Bryant out on his lack of muscle mass, "What you gonna do, you boney ass security guard," while simultaneously raising his fists; I could only hold back my laugh. But on May 6, 2016 our security guard was off duty, I remember because he and I would tag team the metal detector in the morning, where we would empty the contents of Dora the explorer and Batman backpacks, and slide them down the lunch table after the kids walked through the detector. But on this morning I was without his dry sense of humor. Another thing out of the ordinary was that one of my colleagues suggested I try out this new chicken joint off James H. McGee Blvd. and West Third Street. I rarely packed lunch, and had grown tired of my usual, JJ's chicken, so it was a forgone conclusion that I'd be headed there on my lunch break. When I returned to WOW, I was eager to get back into my office to enjoy my meal. I attempted to speed past the students on the playground as they could never resist asking for a piece of whatever I was carrying, "What's up Mr. Payne, oooh give me some of your lunch." After dodging their requests, I landed in my office where I could peacefully enjoy this three-strip chicken breast combo and side of wedges. No less than three minutes later our secretary, Mrs. Hunter, stormed into my office and said, "So y'all just hanging out eating chicken while the school is on lockdown." I gave her a puzzled look, I had not the slightest clue what she was talking about, "A little girl has been stabbed," she exclaimed. I immediately rushed out my office and into the main hallway where I found our principal with a look of sadness that I will never forget. It was one of those days you never quite forget and always replay. The victim was a 2nd grade girl, she was pushed off the swing-set by an anonymous man and attacked with a knife. The other students on the playground ran away screaming which prompted the attention and response from their Teacher. The young girl was rushed to the hospital, while our hearts sank to the pits of our stomachs. I was particularly distraught; I had literally just walked past these kids on that same playground carrying my lunch on my way in the building. On the tape, the animal walked onto school premises, pushed the girl off the swings and stabbed her twice. On a different camera, exactly 51 seconds before the stabbing I can be seen walking into the building carrying a bag of chicken. For months I beat myself up over this day. I'm positive that the assailant waited until I was in the building before he attacked. I'm not sure how things would have ended that day had I witnessed a man stab one of my kids. This story luckily ended with the full recovery of the little girl, and a sigh of relief for an entire school district. But majority of our stories and children are not so lucky. Like one of my favorite students James Banks, who was gunned down at the age of fourteen while sitting in his apartment. I remember sharing pizza with him in my office, letting him come into the gym to hoop when he needed to blow off some steam, or was kicked out of his homeroom. A beautiful brown prince had his life senselessly snatched away before he was even able to understand how precious life is. His life will not be the subject of a 30 for 30 like Benji Wilson, a promising young hoop star from Chicago that was also killed due to senseless gun violence at a tinder age. Nor will it make headlines like other high-profile murders, but he was a young man with all of the potential in the world bottled up in his essence, only to be taken away by the violence of the streets. Remember my friend Tyre from Geometry class, he was also gunned down in his home last year, in front of his young son in west Dayton. Maybe you remember Eric Raglin, my first encounter with a bully, he was found gunned down inside of a white Honda Civic last year in west Dayton. What about my friend Dante', in 2017 he was shot in the chest by his own cousin over an argument in west Dayton, he was pronounced dead at the scene. These are just a few of the lives that have been lost in Dayton, Ohio, a city that has been plagued by exorbitant gun violence, a nationally recognized opioid epidemic, declining economic opportunity, deindustrialization, population decline, pervasive segregation, white flight, urban renewal, systemic poverty, generational poverty, and historically underfunded public schools. A city that was once at the apex of manufacturing, growth, and innovation.

"Why is it that there is a gun shop on almost every corner in this community. Why? Because they want us to kill ourselves. The best way you can destroy a people you take away their ability to reproduce themselves"

Furious Styles - Boyz in the Hood

Econocide

"When I look at project building's, I see slave ships, seaborn vessels
merely turned on their side, and covered with African blood red bricks
to complete the disguise"
Joshua Bennett - We are Poets

I had heard the term gentrification ten years ago, but never really understand what it meant. Once I researched gentrification, I realized all of the ills that I attributed to Dayton were not just distinctive to my community but could be found in majority of urban communities across the country. Areas like Over-The-Rhine (OTR), an urban neighborhood adjacent to downtown Cincinnati, Ohio. In OTR low-income African-Americans are being displaced from a community they have long called home. These African-Americans settled in OTR after the destruction of their previous neighborhood, the West End. Through many urban renewal projects, including the extension of Interstate-75, former West-End residents needed shelter. Many of those residents found cheap housing in a part of town that nobody wanted, OTR. OTR was a dead zone, and developers didn't even bother to practice urban renewal in that area, despite its proximity to downtown. Today the Cincinnati "nonprofit" organization 3CDC, is primarily responsible for the urban renewal in OTR, including the rise of luxury condominiums, expensive apartments, art galleries, yoga studios, and gourmet restaurants. The African-American residents of OTR have been labeled as lazy, jobless, and homeless. The truth is that these residents have been ostracized and denied access to the resurgence that is occurring in their neighborhood. Very little space has been created for mixed-income housing, low-income housing, or supportive housing amiss this redevelopment. The wealthy interests of Cincinnati are focused on creating an extension of luxury from Paul Brown Stadium and the Great American Ballpark, while removing the individuals who do not generate the tax revenue necessary to support this renewed image. This gentrification or "urban renewal" is not exclusive to Cincinnati but is central to many urban communities across America and abroad.

Cleveland and Cincinnati, Ohio have some of the highest rates of childhood poverty in the nation, with Cleveland's being the worst of any large U.S city according to data from the 2016 U.S Census Bureau. Despite being two of the four C's cities in which Miami University heavily recruits, I have not encountered many students from those particular distressed inner-city areas during my time at the University. I never realized how intricately connected every aspect of my life had been to this system of oppression. I now know how powerful policy has been in shaping the world around me. Policy that can forge a survivor's mentality into a mother, even amiss the most natural order of predestined love. Policy that can drive a woman to procreate for the added benefit of an extra social security number, a child support check, and a few tax deductions.

"Y'all don't quote me on this. You start out in 1954 by saying, "Nigger, nigger, nigger." By 1968 you can't say "nigger"—that hurts you. Backfires. So you say stuff like forced busing, states' rights and all that stuff. You're getting so abstract now that you're talking about cutting taxes, and all these things you're talking about are totally economic things and a byproduct of them is that blacks get hurt worse than whites."

Lee Atwater - Campaign strategist to Ronald Reagan

FHA

During the 1930's President Franklin D. Roosevelt wanted to give U.S citizens economic relief through a collection of Federal programs entitled, *The New Deal*. The New Deal was largely responsible for the construction of the modern-day suburbs. Before the New Deal, low-income/middle class blacks and whites lived together in slum areas throughout the United States. The New Deal's original housing initiative was to alleviate the nation's housing shortage, and to provide housing for individuals who had the economic means but could not secure housing. However, this goal shifted to an insidious plan to inculcate people of color into a position of vulnerability. To address the housing shortage, the Federal Government funded the construction of project housing complexes, that initially addressed the housing needs of both blacks and whites. The Federal Housing Administration (FHA) was birthed from the 1934 Federal Housing Act. The Federal Housing Act was a collaboration of Government with private developers to insure mortgages for white families, allowing whites to leave the public housing projects and build a new society in the suburbs. The only requirement for the guarantee of these mortgages was that no loans be written for African-Americans, no matter if they had the economic means to qualify or not. When developers were building suburbs like Levittown, the FHA backed home loans for white families, allowing whites to flee from the slummed, racially homogeneous, project housing of the inner-cities. The security of knowing that if a borrower defaulted, the U.S Government would step in to pay the loan allowed developers to build sprawling suburbs throughout the country. The New Deal set a precedent for banks to follow, redlining African-Americans into the ghettos aka the inner-city. The blight attributed to the inner-city is also a result of racially motivated disinvestment. Banks viewed redlined communities as high-risk and began denying loans to small businesses in those areas on that basis. This practice kept urban areas from participating in this new wave of growth and expansion and accelerated the deterioration of predominantly minority communities.

Redlining

: refuse (a loan or insurance) to someone because they live in an area deemed to be a poor financial risk.

The inner-city is euphemism for all of the ills associated with urban life, such as blight, urban decay, underperforming schools, crime, drugs, and heavy police presence. I recently read a powerful book about the history

126

of this housing segregation entitled, *The Color of Law* which does a masterful job of laying out how housing has been used as a tool to strengthen the racial divide in America. Here is an excerpt from the opening.

"The Public Works Administration (PWA) created a pattern of racial segregation that exists even until this day, creating segregation in areas that were once integrated."
Richard Rothstein - The Color of Law

This segregation has persisted throughout the generations, and helped turn Dayton, Ohio into one of the most segregated cities in the United States. While African-Americans were confined to public housing, white flight to the suburbs was subsidized by the Federal Government, this a key contributor to the enormous wealth gap between the black and white race.

"When you're living with rats, roaches, and things like that --that's deplorable"
Karen Holliday - Baltimore Resident

War on Drugs

"You will be put away and put away for good, three strikes and you are out"
President Bill Clinton

Racial segregation allowed for the continued legal discrimination of African-Americans during the Jim Crow and Civil Rights era, which led to the disproportionate criminalization of African-Americans during the War on Drugs. President Nixon announced the War on Drugs on June

127

18, 1971 and set the stage for decades of targeted destruction of poor, vulnerable minority communities across the country. It is much easier to fight a war against an enemy that is concentrated, confined, and zoned into designated areas of a city. Bill Clinton's 1994 Crime Bill aka, *"Three Strikes"* helped fuel a drastic boom of incarceration and prompted the explosion of the prison industry. The over-policing precedent in poor, minority communities and rising number of convictions birthed the private prison industry. A culture of legal discrimination was created, local police forces were militarized, which led to further destabilization of urban black communities. The war on drugs was targeted towards African-Americans, and other vulnerable communities of color.

"The Clinton administrations 'tough on crime' policies resulted in the largest increase in federal and state prison inmates of any president in American history"
Michelle Alexander - The New Jim Crow

The mandatory minimum sentencing policy was a devastating blow to communities that were already waving the flag of surrender. This policy removed discretionary power away from Judges and forced an over-sentencing precedent for non-violent drug offenses that incarcerated hundreds of thousands of African-Americans and other minorities. Michelle Alexander, a powerful voice in the fight against mass incarceration states that there are more African-American men in prison today, than were on plantations in 1856. Even for individuals who are not physically locked into cages, they remain slaves to the criminal justice system through discriminatory hiring practices such as, "Check the box." The 100:1 crack vs. cocaine disparity was another racially motivated policy intended to disproportionately impact communities of color. During the 1980's, the media hyper sensationalized crack as the drug that will make you kill your own mother. While Caucasians were using cocaine in board rooms, African-Americans were using crack on street corners. The rationale that Congress's used to justify this 100:1

128

sentencing disparity has been debunked by the research data. But even then it was blatantly clear that this policy, and the War on Drugs was an agenda, fought against a minority group that was no longer needed as the economic engine for the U.S. Yet free labor on the backs of African-Americans never gets old in America, and today many African-American men find themselves working as prison laborers for cents on the dollar.

"We knew we couldn't make it illegal to be either against the war or black, but by getting the public to associate the hippies with marijuana and blacks with heroin, and then criminalizing both heavily, we could disrupt those communities. We could arrest their leaders, raid their homes, break up their meetings, and vilify them night after night on the evening news. Did we know we were lying about the drugs? Of course we did."

John Ehrlichman - President Nixon Advisor

As we continue to see the over-policing and killing of unarmed people of color persist we understand that the system itself has been designed to keep us in a state of oppression. In 2018 the Chicago police participated in assisting the Norfolk Southern Railway company in setting up bait trucks loaded with Nike shoes in impoverished areas. This sting operation was set up following a weekend where 66 people were killed due to gun violence, and not one arrest was made. African-American males have been under attack since the formation of the American police system, a system birthed on the basis of helping wealthy landowners recover and punish their runaway slaves. Below lies some startling statistics from the Bureau of Justice Statistics, NAACP, and American Civil Liberties Union.

- In 1986, before the enactment of federal mandatory minimum sentencing for crack cocaine offenses, the average federal drug sentence for African Americans was 11% higher than for whites. Four years later, the average federal drug sentence for African Americans was 49% higher.

- In 2003, whites constituted 7.8% and African Americans constituted more than 80% of the defendants sentenced under the harsh federal crack cocaine laws, despite the fact that more than 66% of crack cocaine users in the United States are white or Hispanic.

- One in three black men can expect to go to prison in their lifetime

- African Americans are incarcerated at more than 5 times the rate of whites

- Black and Hispanic students face harsher punishments in school that lead to youth incarceration

- Today people of color make up 30% of the U.S population but 60% of the prison population

- African Americans and whites use drugs at similar rates, but the imprisonment rate of African Americans is almost 6 times that of whites

Compared to the 22% decrease in crime rates from 1975 to 2002, incarceration rates in the United States increased 323%
(King, Mauer and Young)

In 1990 Congress decided it needed more information on the impact of mandatory sentences, and directed the Sentencing Commission to study mandatory minimums and to report on their effects. In August 1991, the commission completed an in-depth study on mandatory minimums and concluded that non-whites were much more likely to receive mandatory minimum sentences and that they were being applied in a discriminatory manner.
American Civil Liberties Union - Cracks in the System

Rather than dedicate more resources to impoverished schools, cops were placed inside of inner-city schools, helping facilitate the school-prison-pipeline. The result of racially discriminatory policies is economic abandonment, communities left with concentrated poverty, and public schools without the tax revenue necessary to adequately support and prepare students. This is why the school districts in the suburbs are stronger, and produce more students that are "college material," the properties in those communities are worth more, the families pay higher taxes, therefore the schools have more funding, and the students have teachers who are paid a competitive wage. Teachers in affluent communities are not forced to drive Uber or bag groceries following a long day of teaching, and the parents in those suburbs have a voice in their local politics. Majority of urban public schools are not equipped to prepare students for this new technological economy.

Sometimes the term inner-city describes the neighborhoods directly adjacent to downtown, sometimes it describes areas miles away from the city centre, but it always usually synonymous with people of color concentrated in an area that has been economically distressed and generational disinvestment. When you are black and grow up in poverty, surrounded by a dying community, it is far less likely that you will wind up on the campus of an elite institution of higher education, poised for a six-figure job offer from an investment banking firm upon graduation. This is the reality of growing up black in America, in the inner-city.

"In this America, millions of young people grow up in the sunlight of opportunity."
Dr. Martin Luther King Jr. - The Other America

"We can only understand life backwards, but we must live life forward"
Soren Kierkegaard

Rise Above

She said she just finish school, could barely pay tuition

Now she teachin 7 grade, tryna make a difference

But the kids frustrate her, she said they don't listen

An ass like that, how the f*** they supposed to pay attention?

I'm f***in wit you but for real she said they hopeless, a class full of jokesters

Creatin all the obstacles, impossible to focus

Little niggas barely read, tryna give em what they need

And they don't even try, one little boy, he caught her eye

Cuz he looked just like her brother, she be havin to call his mother

But she act like she don't care,

What father? He ain't here

Now she frustrated, thinking that she just made the mistake of her life

Underpaid, be havin to waitress at night

Six years of college down the drain

Drinking, tryna drown the pain

Party with her girls, feelin sorry for the world

Cuz ain't no hope for the youth

Well, ain't that the truth?

When all your role models either rappin or they hoop, damn...

J. Cole - Rise Above

Rest in Power

Ashley James - Dayton, Ohio

Jessie Tyre Chivers Sr. - Dayton, Ohio

James Banks Jr. - Dayton, Ohio

Dante' Jones - Dayton, Ohio

Eric Raglin - Dayton, Ohio

John Crawford - Dayton, Ohio

Kylen English - Dayton, Ohio

Tamir Rice - Cleveland, Ohio

Timothy Thomas - Cincinnati, Ohio

Michael Brown - Ferguson, Missouri

Jassmine McBride - Flint, Michigan

Jazmine Barnes - Houston, Texas

Trayvon Martin - Sanford, Florida

Sandra Bland - Waller County, Texas

Eric Garner - Staten Island, New York

Philando Castile - Falcon Heights, Minnesota

Laquan McDonald - Chicago, Illinois

Sam DuBose - Cincinnati, Ohio

Alton Sterling - Baton Rouge, Louisiana

Freddie Gray - Baltimore, Maryland

Oscar Grant - Oakland, California

Jordan Davis - Jacksonville, Florida

Latasha Harlins - Los Angeles, California

ShoMari Payne

Cliff Dixon - Atlanta, Georgia

And to every other person that lost their life as a pawn to systemic oppression, senseless gun violence, police brutality, and intentional economic abandonment

ACT III
STRENGTH BY NECESSITY

"Because what is learned out of necessity is inevitably more powerful

than the learning that comes easily"

Malcolm Gladwell

This phase of the book is dedicated to training our endurance and strength. We will dive into the science of exercise, explore health statistics, examine sports performance, and revisit historical testaments of endurance in the face of tribulation. Without endurance we become nameless victims, allowing the circumstances of life to overcome our power and boundless potential. Endurance is required to withstand the great forces and pressures of life. We will explore how endurance harnesses our light, so that it may sustain us through our darkest nights and lead us to brighter days. Strength is prerequisite required to break the chains of bad habits. Professional athletes innately embody the principle of strength training, it is a large part of their sacrifice which enables them to compete at the highest level. The 5:00 AM morning sprints, the lonely late-night weight room sessions, and strict dietary guidelines are all part of the commitment necessary to fortify mental and physical strength. But I'm going to let you in on a secret, everyone has the potential to become an athlete, it only requires consistent training. The caveat is that it's not easy to build strength, and it's certainly not painless. We shall now begin the second phase of our journey.

Strength
(noun)
: the inherent capacity to manifest energy, to endure, and to resist
: the quality or state of being strong: capacity for exertion or endurance

Endurance
(noun)
: the ability to do something difficult for a long time
: the ability to deal with pain or suffering that continues for a long time
: the ability to withstand hardship or adversity; especially the ability to sustain a prolonged stressful effort or activity

CHAPTER I
The Middle Passage

I believe endurance and strength are the two building blocks necessary to climb the ladder of adversity. Endurance allows us to withstand the currents of life, no matter how hard they may come. The Middle Passage is one of the most powerful examples of sustained endurance in world history. For African-Americans, the Middle Passage was the darkest hour in the long night of American chattel slavery. This period in history has been given the name "Maafa" by Afrocentric Scholars, a Swahili term translated as "Great Disaster" or "terrible occurrence." We commit a mighty injustice to millions of nameless warriors when we omit this chapter from the story of world history. Many current social studies books imply African-American slaves were escorted to the new world by way of cruise line, failing to give reverence to the inner-strength of the enslaved.

> *"The slave ships were delightful, the voyage from Africa to the West Indies was one of the happiest periods of their lives"*
> *Robert Norris - Slave ship Captain*

This inhumane voyage to the Americas was a journey designed to break the spiritual walls of a people. So much so that many slaves leaped overboard rather than face the horrid conditions of the Middle Passage.

Slaves met death by sea at such regularity that sharks in the vast Atlantic Ocean adjusted their swim patterns to mirror those of slave ships. Historians estimate around 10-15% of slaves that were captured from West Africa died during the Middle Passage, totaling around 2 million. For every 100 slaves that reached the New World, another 40 died in Africa or during the Middle Passage. I ache for those lost at sea, my heart fills with sadness when I meditate on the atrocities committed against my ancestors. To be chained, helpless, packed in the bottom of a dark ship was a preview to the lifelong enslavement experienced on American plantations. The conditions endured throughout the voyage was so deadly even the European slave traders had a high mortality rate. Close your eyes for a moment, picture yourself chained to the person to your left and to your right, at the bottom of a boat. The atmosphere is consumed by the smell of fresh vomit, feces, urine, mucus, blood, saliva, and death. You are constantly gasping for oxygen in a packed corridor, but find not one ounce of fresh air. You are exhausted and malnourished, and have decided that death is preferably to life and refuse to eat the slop that is tossed down to you. Your capturer acknowledges your resistance by kicking out your teeth with the heel of his boot and proceeds to force feed you like a hog. It is pitch black, you are clinging to hope that God will rescue you from this hell, yet hell you remain. Many perished simply from being overtaken by this horrific experience, in addition to the rampant illnesses, frequent beatings, mutilations, suicides, and rapes, they also died from melancholy (extreme sadness). I remember reading accounts from slaves who endured the affliction of the middle passage from the book *Slave Ships and Slaving*, by George Francis Dow.

"Don't they have food in the place of bad spirits?"
"One by one the faces I remember from down below were gone, now I only had one friend, death"

Despite this horrific affliction, there were survivors, and I owe my existence to their inner strength and endurance. Where does one find the strength to endure such turmoil? How does one transform the human body to become a vessel capable of enduring this one to six-month inferno across the Atlantic Ocean? I painfully imagine myself packed in the bottom of a slave ship traveling across the Atlantic, with my ancestors gasping for air. Accounts from various captain's log tell us that temperatures were so hot in the slave holes, sometimes the candles the captains lit wouldn't burn, because there wasn't enough oxygen. Today we disrespect their memory and sacrifice by intentionally destroying our bodies through the cancer that is tobacco. We take oxygen for granted, forgetting that even air was not a commodity afforded to those who endured the horror of the Transatlantic Slave Trade.

CHAPTER II
Oxygen (O2)

"Your back hurt and your neck hurt and you smoking heavy, and I sit next to you and I lecture you because those are deadly"
Drake - Look What You've Done

The lungs are the primary conductor of facilitating oxygen consumption. By definition the lungs are among the hardest-working organs in the body. They expand and contract up to twenty times a minute to supply oxygen that is then distributed to tissues all over the body and expel the carbon dioxide that has been created throughout the body. Carbon Dioxide is the waste product created when you produce energy. Strengthening the lungs is critical to improving overall health and increasing life expectancy. The term "aerobic" means requiring the presence of oxygen. According to the American College of Sports Medicine, any sport or activity that works large groups of muscles, is continually maintained and performed rhythmically, is defined as aerobic, or cardiovascular. Think of jumping jacks and jump rope in middle school, during these aerobic exercises the lungs bring oxygen into the body to provide energy and removes carbon dioxide. The heart then pumps that oxygen to the working muscles that are doing the exercise. Aerobic conditioning trains the heart and lungs to pump blood more efficiently.

"Like the rest of your body, lungs thrive on movement and activity."
Jennifer M. Ryan, PT, MS, DPT

Smoke Screen

From a basic google search you can find enough reasons to put down the cigarettes and pick up the bottle of water. But many African-Americans still can't muster the strength to abandon this deadly habit. Despite the fact smoking cigarettes is linked to shorter life expectancy, increased future medical expenses, and countless other deadly illnesses. Most jobs welcome "smoke breaks" to allow employees a dedicated time to slowly kill themselves. While health insurance companies offer increased premiums for tobacco users. To put it plainly.

Smoking Cigarettes is the single most preventable cause of death in the United States.

Think about that for a moment. People literally work jobs they hate and spend that money on a product that has been proven to kill them, I couldn't think of a worse investment. Tobacco is responsible for around 435,000 deaths per year, or 1 out of 6 deaths in the U.S each year. Throw in another 41,000 deaths due to secondhand smoke exposure, and 20,000 flu and pneumonia deaths are linked to smoking. Every year 174,000 smokers will die from heart disease. Smoking also increases the risk of dying of a heart attack by 60%. Smokers die on average ten years earlier than nonsmokers. So why would anyone increase their risk of death through a preventable activity? The only explanation is that smoking is an addictive habit, by intentional design.

"I freed a thousand slaves, and I could've freed a thousand more if they only knew they were slaves"
Harriet Tubman

We are married to our habits, and we often consider divorce painful and not worth the hassle. Overcoming a detrimental habit requires us to dedicate energy and sacrifice familiarity. Most smokers believe they will be one of the lucky ones unaffected by the glaring statistics. They rationalize their addiction with cliché statements such as, "We all gon die one day." This becomes a comfort zone, and smokers have found more refuge in their own demise, versus implementing the few small adjustments necessary to kick the habit. The threat of change becomes the enemy. And of course, smoking is big business for the medical industry. The 36.5 million smokers will eventually require the medical attention of surgeons, physicians, nurses, pharmacists, medical assistants, etc. Remember this is the number one most preventable cause of death in the U.S. So, one must ask, does the U.S have a financial incentive to end smoking? Absolutely not. The U.S has a bottom line that serves the elite and wealthy, and it is our duty to protect ourselves from the entities that capitalize off of our ignorance. As consumers and citizens, we must collectively combat the concerted efforts of private business and the failures of the Federal Government to protect us against overt genocide. The data on smoking and its effects on human health are clear. If you are a smoker I challenge you to replace cigarettes with another activity. If you are not a smoker, I urge you to become an advocate in the fight against tobacco companies. We are losing the battle every time we allow a relative or friend to smoke their life away for a temporary relief. As an African-American, I am even more sensitive to this epidemic. Tobacco companies are capitalizing on the ignorance of poor and marginalized black citizens in addition to a frustrated working class. Let us rally together in the fight against tobacco companies. Too many of our relatives are being remembered instead of experienced, too much time has been spent lying in hospital beds, and entirely too much money has been invested into our own demise. **You have been challenged.**

"Big Tobacco must love diversity, they love it so much that they advertise 10x more in black neighborhoods than in other neighborhoods"

Amanda Seales truth correspondent

"I know why Newport's got so popular in the black community, doesn't the logo look like a Nike swoosh"
Ali Payne

Tobacco use is a major contributor to the three leading causes of death among African Americans—heart disease, cancer, and stroke.

Centers for Disease Control and Prevention

CHAPTER III
Water (H$_2$O)

New Orleans, Louisiana
August 2005
Ultimately, 80 percent of New Orleans and large portions of nearby parishes became flooded, and the floodwaters did not recede for weeks

One of the most devastating hurricanes in U.S history ravished the shores of Florida, Alabama, Georgia, Mississippi, and Louisiana on August 29, 2005. The final death toll for Hurricane Katrina was 1,836. Forty-percent of the deaths in Louisiana were caused by drowning, twenty-five percent were caused by injury and trauma, and eleven-percent were caused by heart conditions. Ten-thousand people sought shelter from the storm in the Superdome football stadium. Katrina is ranked as the third deadliest Hurricane in American history. The estimated cost of damages from the storm is around $125 billion (2005 USD). Nothing breaks my heart more than this 21st century American tragedy. New Orleans, Louisiana was the area most impacted by this deadly storm. What stands out to me beyond the natural disaster was the aftermath, the failure of the richest nation in the world to come to the aid of their own citizens who were drowning right before their eyes. The images of black and brown bodies seen floating throughout the city, the elderly walking up and down the highway underneath the scorching sun in search for aid. The rampant disease, the unnecessary suffering, and the Superdome which served as shelter and beacon of hope. I remember CNN's Wolf Blitzer standing in his generational suit of privilege calling U.S citizens "refugees." I remembered feeling empowered watching Kanye West stand up for those very citizens when he went off script and said, "George Bush does not care about black people." I've watched Spike Lee's documentary, *When The Levees Broke* over and over, I've read Dr. Michael Eric Dyson's *Come Hell or High Water*, and I've read Dr. Henry Giroux's *Stormy Weather*, all of which help shed light on the true essence of this preventable tragedy. I've read accounts from residents who believe the levees were intentionally detonated, in an attempt to preserve the French Quarter, and ensure the majority of the damage impacted the poor and powerless. Whether this is fact or conjecture, what remains clear is that the forgotten, mostly black and brown residents of New Orleans were in danger long before August 24, 2005 at 11:00 am, when Tropical Storm Katrina was first given her name. They were victims of a racial hierarchy that has governed blacks since the White Lion slave ship arrived at Point Comfort (Hampton, Virginia). May we never forget what was lost, and the inner strength of those who endured this political disaster.

"Dead bodies, mostly poor Black People, were left uncollected in the streets, on porches, in hospitals, nursing homes, electric wheelchairs and collapsed houses, prompting some people to claim that the United states had become like a "third world country"

Dr. Henry Giroux

American Poverty

Philip Alston is a special rapporteur for the United Nations, he travels the world exposing injustices in third-world countries. Generally, his travels land him in some of the poorest places on the planet. In 2017

Philip Alston visited Lowndes County in Alabama, an area that is concentrated with African-Americans, and is currently spilling open sewage in the front and backyards of the residents. Roughly half of the homes in Lowndes county have failing septic systems, or do not have septic systems at all. Without a septic tank waste from the residents home literally flows from a pipe and into the lawn. The racial disparity is apparent in Lowndes County, where white residents in the county were provided with septic tanks from their respective city municipalities decades ago. This failure of government to provide basic necessities to residents with some of the highest poverty rates in the country is heartbreaking.

In the town of Reserve, Louisiana residents suffer from a cancer rate that is 700-800 times higher than the rest of the United States, it has been named the Cancer Capital of the country. Reserve, Louisiana lies between New Orleans and Baton Rouge, and is filled with African-American residents that have little economic mobility or social capital. The obvious culprit for the astronomically high cancer rates is the presence of larger chemical plants in the region like DuPont. The Environmental Protection Agency (EPA) identified Chloroprene as a carcinogen, an emission that the DuPont plant emits during its production process, it is the only factory in the United States that emits this chemical. The Chloroprene that is emitted during production is used to go into Neoprene material that goes into wetsuits and laptop covers.

Flint, Michigan

If you were around in 2014 your probably heard about the water crisis in Flint, Michigan. Like other rust-belt cities Flint suffered from the decline of the car industry, lack of economic diversity, white flight, and failed local government. Flint was once a booming U.S city, with a peak population of around 200,000 in the 1960's, today the population of Flint is around 96,000. In 2011, Flint officials made a financial decision that will forever leave lasting scars on its residents. The State of Michigan developed the position "Emergency Managers", these individuals were empowered to make cost-cutting decisions without going through the typical political process. The Mayor and the city

144

council were removed from Flint and other municipalities throughout Michigan in an effort to "save money". In April 2014, Flint officials, specifically the Emergency Manager made the deadly decision to cease purchasing water from Detroit, Michigan (Lake Huron), and to join a new regional water system as a cost-saving measure. While waiting to join the new water network, the city decided to use water from the Flint river. Immediately following the switch, residents began complaining about the taste, smell, and color of the water, but the city refuted these initial complaints. An outside investigation by Virginia Tech researchers revealed what Flint residents already knew, their water showed higher than normal levels of lead. The slow response and initial denial of the crisis by city officials resulted in Flint effectively poisoning its citizens. All 8,000 children under six years old were poisoned by the water. The Flint water crisis was linked to a rise in E.coli and legionnaires disease, at least 12 people were killed, and at least 91 people became ill, along with long-term consequences for the children who were exposed to the higher lead levels, and a significant increase in fetal death rates during the crisis. The failure of the Government to protect its citizens is not foreign to African-Americans. We have been the chattel of this rich nation since before its 1776 inception, but today race is no longer the sole precursor for being disposable, the lack of wealth can place anyone in a state of vulnerability. The only way to combat these forces is to fortify ourselves, to sharpen our minds and bodies against the greed and forces of capitalism. The poor in this country have always been disposable, but we can train ourselves to overcome, just as those before us have done in the face of adversity and injustice.

CHAPTER IV
Exercise

"Muscle is created by repeatedly lifting things that have been designed

to weigh us down"

Rudy Francisco

What is exercise? Exercise is a controlled form of stress on the body. For exercise to produce change, there must be enough stress to trigger a physiological response. In other words, if you aggressively challenge the body, it has the ability to respond, adapt, and improve. We stress the body through consistent physical training, followed by rest and recovery, followed by an adaption to the stimulus, and finally we return with more strength and endurance. You must continue to progressively challenge the body for continuous change. Progressive training must be of the appropriate intensity, too little intensity and your body will feel no need to adapt, too much stress and you risk injury. On the surface exercise is just a physical activity, it could be running, jumping, pushing, pulling, lifting, carrying, cycling, swimming, stretching, yoga, etc. But if we look deeper, we see that exercise has many benefits that truly can make us live happier and healthier lives. And if we look even deeper, we see that exercise reveals a lot about who we are, what we can be, and our internal values. The act of self-punishment is admittedly tough, and the fear of physical pain can turn New Year's resolutions into the annual lies we tell ourselves. Most people are aware that exercise facilitates weight loss and can help us achieve a more aesthetic physique, but the greatest impact of exercise is on our long-term health. The U.S claims one of the highest obesity rates in the world. However, many U.S fast food chains are now exporting their operations to developing parts of the world as America grows increasingly health conscious. According to the *Economist* publication, the number of overweight children under five in Africa has increased by 50%. In the U.S one in three Americans are obese, and two out of every three citizens are classified as overweight. How is this possible in the land of

146

Planet Fitness, LA Fitness, 24 Hour Fitness, Anytime Fitness, Community Recreation Centers, YMCA, P90X, Insanity, Instagram trainers, etc.? As a Certified Strength & Conditioning Specialist, ACE Certified Personal Trainer, and TRX Certified Group Instructor I will give you my anecdotal answer, because we are tired. I am guilty of countless lapses towards my exercise goals, and those lapses have lasted weeks, months, and even over a year. Pursuing higher education, working full-time, fast-food, family time, sleep, and personal relationships have all factored into why I have under-prioritized my health & fitness goals over the past year. Even finishing this book has taken priority, but realistically I have no excuse, and neither do you, but I do believe we are all fatigued.

"It's easy to do what's convenient, but what's convenient isn't always the

right thing"

Xan Barksdale

Fatigue

fatigue - **extreme** tiredness, typically resulting from mental or physical exertion or illness.

Why are we so fatigued? Many of us are fatigued from life, not necessarily our workout regimens. Fatigue during exercise occurs during both short-term and prolonged exercise. The energy and power generated by contracting muscles depletes the body energy stores and sensations of fatigue and exhaustion appear. The relationship between exercise and fatigue has always been an area of interest in the field of exercise science. Research studies reveal that fatigue occurs when certain substances accumulate, or others become depleted. During a resting state, the muscles store carbohydrates in the form of glycogen. When you perform exercise, your body breaks down this stored glycogen and turns it into usable energy. Depletion of muscle glycogen is generally the primary cause of fatigue, although your muscles can exercise two hours or more at a continuous high-intensity pace before fatigue begins. Intermittent or lower-intensity exercise uses up stored glycogen much more slowly, delaying fatigue. Most athletes performing prolonged high-intensity exercises consume sugar-containing drinks to avoid fatigue. Fatigue is a byproduct of hard work, intensity, and sustained effort. Rest is a necessary component of recovery, and the best-known antidote for fatigue. Professional athletes take rest days, where they do not engage in any physical activity associated with their sport, you too should create a similar template for your own life, prioritizing exercise and rest.

Resistance

"Band work, prehab and joint mobility is important, but at some point you need to load the body with real resistance"
J.J Reddick - Philadelphia 76ers

Resistance training is one of the most proven methods of enhancing muscular growth. Lifting weights, adding resistance to the treadmill, or strapping on a weight vest before your set of pull-ups are all ways of increasing the intensity of your workout session. A 2018 study performed by Dr. Wael Jaber a cardiologist from the Cleveland Clinic discovered that a sedentary lifestyle is worse for your health than smoking, diabetes, and heart disease. The other revelation from this research study was that fitness leads to a longer life, with no upper-limit for risk for "ultra-exercisers." This study helps us all understand that not exercising is no longer an option, not if we want to live a long and healthy life. Exercise is the prescription we need to cure our sedentary culture and move the needle forward towards a more energetic existence.

"We're meant to walk, run, exercise. It's all about getting up and moving."
Dr. Satjit Bhusri - Cardiologist at Lenox Hill Hospital

Use it or Lose it

Atrophy: gradual loss of muscle or flesh usually because of disease or lack of use.: A wasting away or progressive decline.

Atrophy is a term used to describe a gradual loss of muscle. When you commit to the journey of building physical strength your muscles will hypertrophy, a fancy scientific term that means grow in size. When you cease resistance training, your body slowly begins to decrease protein synthesis and your hard-earned muscle mass will gradually atrophy or decrease in size. When a person breaks a bone and the bone is placed in a cast, the muscle is inactive, which facilitates atrophy. For astronauts, the process of atrophy is accelerated. On earth a woman over 50 who is untreated for bone loss can lose 2% of hip bone mass in one year, in space astronauts can lose that same amount in a single month. Muscle mass and strength can be reduced as much as 20-40% during long duration missions. Astronauts exercise up to 2.5 hours a day, six days a week to minimize the negative effects of spaceflight on their bodies, they literally have to fight the expedited atrophy process through exercise. In an age of instant gratification, the timeless adage of old-fashioned exercise holds true. This process is the same for mental atrophy.

"Reading is to the mind, what exercise is to the body"
Unknown

When we begin to limit our visions and cease stretching our imaginations beyond our current level, we will experience mental atrophy, and over time our physical surroundings will reflect this mental laziness and complacency. We must consistently push the envelope of creativity; to ensure that we remain the narrators of our own unique stories. Have you ever known someone who never decided to break the pattern of mental atrophy? A person who never took risks, accepted the status quo, and remained nonchalant towards their deepest desires? This thinking is dangerous because it is a common illusion of the masses. Only to wake up one day and find that you have accumulated decades of habits and consequences along your drift. I'm reminded of a story I read in Raymond Holliwell's classic book, *Working With The Law*.

THE WOMAN WHO WANTED A SMALL ROOM

I knew a woman who once lived in a beautiful home in an exclusive suburban district with every comfort that wealth could supply to make her happy. This home was a large rambling house, facing a beautiful lake, with green terraces sloping to its edge. Flower gardens, perfectly kept, were scattered freely along each path throughout the estate. She had many servants to help her, and from observation her life was just about as complete as one might dream about. But, with all this wealth and beauty, the woman was heard to remark to her friends that she hoped the day would come when she would be relieved of the big house and all its problems and could live in a trunk. She wanted a room to herself, for herself, and just large enough to move about without any extra space to dust and to keep clean. A few years elapsed. Her husband died and left the estate to her. She sold the home at a sacrifice. Her other holdings depreciated so much in value through unwise investments and transfers that she had but a small income left. She went to live with a sister, and, true to her wish, she now has a small room on the third floor and practically lives in a trunk. Whether she is happier now than before I do not know, but I doubt it. One thing I do know; that is, she gradually led herself to the small room and privations when her consciousness began to grow small and limited. She unconsciously touched the creative principle and supplied it with ideas of smallness and privacy and limitation which materialized within a few years' time.

Raymond Holliwell – Working With The Law
(Footnote)

CHAPTER V
Repetitions

Repetition
:the recurrence of an action or event.

When sports analyst praise athlete's versatility, they usually are referring to an athlete's ability to play multiple positions, not multiple sports. But long before he was being praised on Monday Night Football for making the transition from Division 1 small forward to NFL starting offensive lineman, I knew Fant had a shot in the NFL. George Fant played four years of college basketball at WKU and used his last year of Division 1 sports eligibility to pivot into an entirely new sport, football. Fant did not tear up the gridiron with his statistics during his lone season of football at WKU, as he hadn't played football since the 8th grade. During his final year of sports eligibility Fant appeared in 12 games and caught one pass for seven yards. But Fant spent the entire year training with the WKU Strength and Conditioning staff in preparation to shock pro scouts at the NFL combine. Western Kentucky University does not boast world class training staff or facilities like The Ohio State University, Duke, University of North Carolina, or the University of Alabama. Many of my fellow WKU alumni that made splashes in professional sports like Bobby Rainey, George Fant, Courtney Lee, Brandon Doughty, and Antonio Andrews use repetitions as their advantage. The lack of entertainment in a place like Bowling Green, Kentucky can bode well when one's desire is to focus on upgrading skills and abilities. This is the advantage of the underdog that Malcolm Gladwell refers to as Big Fish, Little Pond, or the desirable disadvantage. Developmental biologist Dr. Bruce Lipton puts it this way, "The way to train your subconscious mind is through repetition." The key to mastering exercise, piano, your job, a new language, or any upgrade to your life is through the boring process of putting in the reps. Fant found it more advantageous to study the game of football, than double down on basketball. He made the decision to prepare himself for the one thing that was within his control, the NFL combine.

"Whatever you set your mind to"
George Fant

Resilience

Resilience
1: capable of withstanding shock without permanent deformation or rupture
2: tending to recover from or adjust easily to misfortune or change

" To understand the kind of mindset that could turn a failure into a gift"

Dr. Carol Dweck

Growing up I always questioned why God placed me in such difficult circumstances. I would spend weekends in Vandalia, Ohio reading the bible with Grandpa Payne, then return back to Dayton and wonder why my prayers for a bed, and a better life went unanswered. I began to hate Gloria, because I realized that the design of my environment was intentional. Intentional because she forced me to sleep right there on the living room floor, next to the kitchen which was the scariest place in the house. The kitchen where the mice traps would go off throughout the night interrupting my sleep, the kitchen where hundreds of roaches would be scattered across the counter top at any given moment. My pallet was strategically placed next to the room I rarely dared to enter, especially after nightfall. Gloria refused to clean out any room so that I could at least be away from the chaos in the kitchen, she ensured that my pallet was right next to the action. As a child I often heard cliché phrases in church such as, "God gives his toughest battle to his strongest warriors," or "The Lord won't put more on you than you can bear." These are powerful statements indeed, but they mean very little to a seven-year-old boy sleeping on the floor, hungry, in a filthy house overrun by mice and roaches. What I have learned is that if it weren't for my resilience, I would have succumbed to the circumstances, and manifested the outcome intended by my oppressor.

CHAPTER VI
Desirable Disadvantage

"Strength doesn't come from winning. Your struggles develop your

strength. When you go through hardships and decide not to surrender,

that is strength"

Mahatma Gandhi

Our society tends to operate under the assumption that everyone comes from the same starting place in life, which makes it easier for comparisons. This is why I praise Malcolm Gladwell's important book, *Outliers* as it was a foundational text that describes how we allow others to shape our perceptions of success. Maybe I didn't score lower than William on the ACT exam because I am less intelligent, but because I went to sleep hungry for the last three nights and I was barely focused during the exam. Maybe everyone's parents do not make six figures and can afford for them to attend summer SAT boot camps, afford tutors, and supply nutritious meals. Sociologist Annette Lareau studied 3rd graders in a long-term ethnographic study and concluded that having involved parents was the key difference that leads to an individual's success in life. Everyone comes to the game of life equipped differently, what the underdog must learn is that everything must be used as fuel, the margin for error is much smaller when climbing from the pits of poverty and striving for greatness. Malcolm Gladwell identified that a statistically significant number of CEOs "suffer" from dyslexia, highlighting that this perceived disadvantage can be flipped on its head. Anecdotally, I have witnessed that my relatives who never escape the poverty mindset have fallen victim to materialism. Too many of us measure success in our possessions, the fullness of our closets, the year and make of our automobile, and the square feet in our home. But true growth resides in overcoming the old self. When is the last time you set a true internal challenge for yourself? Such as setting out to learn a new language, learn to play an instrument, register for a course at the local community college, read a new book, write a book, or wake up early to work out for a month straight? These internal victories mean much more in the metaphysical realm than we could realize in the moment. Is success about the number of zeros in someone's bank account? Is the man who has sat on his couch for 10 years watching Maury successful because he hit the lottery? Is he more successful than the fatherless child who has forged their own way into a meaningful life? Do not tie your self-worth to money or material things, only the advancement of your current situation. This is why I love the metaphor of exercise, because the once inconceivable such as losing 500lbs, can be accomplished through effort, hard work, and consistency.

"Opportunity is missed by most people because it is dressed in overalls and looks like work"

Thomas Edison

True achievement lies in discarding the greed mentality instilled by the western world, drowning out the noise, and listening to the voice within. I believe the bible states it this way, "Place your treasures not on Earthly things where thieves steal." This metaphor teaches us that our material possessions are not of universal importance, we are bigger than them all. The great Muhammad Ali once said, "The greatest victory in life is to rise above the material things we once valued most." You are not your 401K, Apple Watch, Dodge Charger, your hourly wage or salary. I remind myself of these crucial facts daily, because materialism is a game you can never really win. Will you buy the new 2020 Porsche after you just purchased the 2019? And the 2021 model the year after that? I highly doubt you would make such a foolish investments, but you can certainly set out to run one more marathon this year than last, lower your blood pressure, invest in a start-up business in your community, donate an organ to a loved one or total stranger, challenge yourself physically and mentally, sharpen yourself and those around you, read a book a week, write that book you've been talking about, and achieve that dream you allowed yourself to believe was unachievable. The famed speaker Les Brown says, "Pull out your check stubs and see how much you sold your soul for." Did you hear about the people who committed suicide during the 2008 recession? In what world does a human being become so engulfed in their financial status that losing it no longer motivates them to try again, but to end their life altogether? According to a 2014 Forbes article, the 2008 economic downturn is linked to more than 10,000 suicides across North America and Europe. I'm sure many of these people suffered from other issues, but financial adversity helped position them into a deadly corner, but you are different. You understand that trial and triumph are both part of the harmony of life. You understand that better is a book (knowledge) than a well-built house (material possession). You are motivated by setbacks because you understand that adversity provides the necessary steps to climb the mountain of success. You have learned to see the silver lining in every situation. You have built highways to bypass the congested lanes of mopers and declined RSVPs to pity parties. You have built such a strong foundation that even when life sends a hurricane against your shores, you emerge from the storm stronger and more resilient.

CHAPTER VII
Strength

"You and I know what's the best way to keep the nigger from voting,

and you do it the night before the election."

Theodore Bilbo - Mississippi senator/Klansman

I have always been obsessed with the Civil Rights era, this fascination stems from my childhood conversations with my Grandma. The black and white photos from the Civil Rights movement speak to me in a way that is both prophetic and nostalgic. Maybe because I can literally see my Grandma in that struggle, and thus see a part of myself. I often imagine what role I would have played in the fight for freedom. Would I have been a follower of Malcolm X, with an unwavering stance on interracial commerce, militia, and brotherhood? Or a follower of King, methodical, calculated, and nonviolent? Nevertheless, I have studied this time from various perspectives and traveled to countless museums searching for the answers to that very question. I have interviewed my great aunts and uncles who all grew up in Munford, Alabama during the 1930's and 1940's, searching for their intimate experiences and feelings surrounding their upbringing. Some of Grandma Clark's siblings migrated north seeking refuge from the terror of the South, only to find ourselves in a more sophisticated form of racial oppression. Some stayed in the South, in the trenches of the overt horrors of racial oppression. They witnessed the bombing of 16th Street Baptist Church in 1963, they felt the weight of the Medgar Evers assassination, and the brutal beating of Emmett Till. They heard from their parents about the Tulsa Race Riot that killed over 300 African-Americans and brought the wealthiest black community in the country to ashes. I recently began studying infamous housing projects, such as Cabrini Green and Robert Taylor projects in Chicago, the infamous Pruitt Igoe projects of St. Louis, the Brewster Douglass Projects of Detroit, and the Barry Farm projects of D.C. This study shed much light on the story of African-Americans following WWII. As I discussed in ACT II, the public housing system has played a key role in the prosperity for one half of society, and systemic stagnation for the other

.

"That's why it's a black market, that's why it's called the trap, that's

why it's called the projects 'cause it's exactly that"

JAY-Z

I can relate to those individuals who were packed inside those project housing structures, although I did not grow up in a tower with faulty elevators during the crack era, I intimately feel connected to that particular struggle. I've laid next to the rats, unintentionally ate a cockroach that crawled in my oatmeal, and slept in a dwelling the size of a parking space. I often imagine how might I have turned out had I been born in 1955, and raised in Chicago's Stateway Gardens, an area that was one of the poorest in America at the time. Maybe I would have become a petty dealer, a bully, a notorious gang member, or gunned down around the corner from my high school like Benji Wilson. Where you live impacts where you attend school, how many grocery stores and jobs are in your community, the infrastructure, the way the police treat you, and ultimately is a large predictor of your destiny. To endure what African-Americans and other minorities have faced in this country since before its inception requires grit, resilience, and strength. I know no stronger race of people stronger, or a story more triumphant. Despite the blistering Atlantic voyage, chains, rape, nooses, terror, Ku Klux Klan, COINTELPRO, assassinations, fire-hoses, gentrification, housing-projects, pollution, failed government, discrimination, racist policies, and police brutality, we have withstood it all.

"There are two ways of exerting one's strength: one is pushing down,

the other is pulling up"

Booker T. Washington

The land of my birth welcomes me to her shores only as a slave, and spurns with contempt the idea of treating me differently.
So that I am an outcast from the society of my childhood, and an outlaw in the land of my birth. "I am a stranger with thee, and a sojourner as all my fathers were."
That men should be patriotic is to me perfectly natural; and as a philosophical fact, I am able to give it an intellectual recognition. But no further can I go. If ever I had any patriotism, or any capacity for the feeling, it was whips out of me long since by the lash of the American soul-drivers

Frederick Douglass

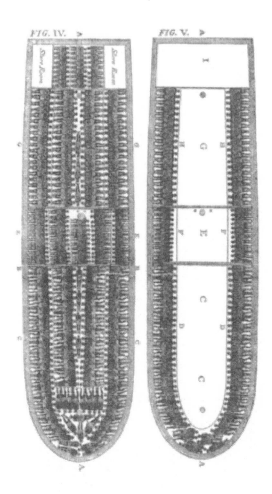

ACT IV
Pain is a Stimulus

In the previous chapter we examined the immense potential of the physical body and its transformative power through a scientific lens. In this final chapter we will marry the physical capabilities of the body, with the boundless potential of the mind. We will explore the law of attraction, the power of mental visualization, and physical manifestation; revealing the critical reality, that our mind is the supreme conductor of our physical circumstances. The power of our thoughts should never be underestimated. We will explore personal testaments to this power in attempt to quantify this age-old adage, *"As a man thinketh, so is he."* Before I sat for the ACT exam, I invested weeks imagining myself on the campus of Western Kentucky University. Little did I know, through these tiny actions, combined with physical effort, I was manifesting my desired outcome. I transformed seventeen years of pain into a new physical reality.

"Up from a past that's rooted in pain I rise"

Maya Angelou

Pain
: a basic bodily sensation induced by
a noxious stimulus, received by naked nerve
endings, characterized by physical discomfort,
and typically leading to evasive **action**...

Stimulus
: something that causes something else to happen, develop,
or become more **active**
: something that causes a change or a reaction

159

CHAPTER I
Dreamville

Throughout my childhood I found it very difficult to hold onto a dream. Most nights when I laid my head on the floor, I was paranoid, anxiously awaiting the sound of a mice trap to go off in the kitchen. I was focused on the roaches crawling up and down the walls, constantly moving and fidgeting trying to ensure nothing crawled on me while I laid on the floor. For a dream to reach actualization it requires nurturing, fuel, and consistent positive affirmation. Every day when I arrived home from school I analyzed my environment, and I was constantly reminded that I was not in a land of dreams, but a field of trash and oppression. The most disheartening aspect of my upbringing was that nothing ever changed, and that my prayers went seemingly unanswered. No moving company rolled in a bed for me during my senior year of high school, no exterminator with a big puffy suit eliminated the roaches or rats, and extreme home makeover never demolished my nightmare, and built us a beautiful new dream home, we just stayed there, night after night, year after year. You don't even have a desk to sit and write your dreams down, I would often think to myself. At the time, I didn't allow my pain to become my stimulus, I allowed my pain to prevent me from excuse not to dream.

What happens to a dream deferred?

Does it dry up

like a raisin in the sun?

Or fester like a sore—

And then run?

Does it stink like rotten meat?

Or crust and sugar over—

like a syrupy sweet?

Maybe it just sags

like a heavy load.

Or does it explode?

Langston Hughes

Detroit, Michigan

The most accomplished businesswoman I know is my cousin, Pamela Rodgers. Pam is the daughter of Grandpa Payne's sister Yvonne, and we met one thanksgiving in Detroit at her parents' immaculate home. I remember Ali and I being in awe at the sheer size of the home, and all of the trinkets that lied within. There was a massive lake in the backyard, which was frozen at the time, but Ali and I hit golf balls into it like we were a couple of big shots on some corporate outing. This was my first snapshot of black excellence, their house made Grandpa and Grannie Payne's look like the humble Appalachian trailers we would pass when traveling through West Virginia. I digress, but in 1992 Pam became one of the first African-American female car dealership owners in the United States. However, her journey to corporate juggernaut was not a smooth sail. Pam earned her bachelor's degree in Economics at the University of Michigan, and her MBA from the prestigious Fuqua College of Business at Duke University. Pam and I keep up on LinkedIn and despite her full schedule, she always makes herself available to lend professional and personal advice.

"Show me someone content with mediocrity, and I'll show you someone destined for failure."
Pam Rodgers

Upon completing her MBA, Pam landed a dream position as a financial analyst for Ford Motor Company. She excelled and was quickly climbing the corporate ladder. While at Ford she got wind of a Dealer Training Program at General Motors. When she first applied to the dealer training program she was turned down because of her lack of experience. So, she quit her lucrative position as a financial analyst, and began selling cars. She left behind comfortability, ventured into uncertainty, put security in her rearview mirror, and decided to chase a dream.

"I was told business was too tough for women, women were too fragile and could not handle the demands and competitive nature of business"
Pamela Rodgers

In 1993, Pam was given her first opportunity, inheriting a struggling location, Flat Rock Chevrolet Oldsmobile, and later with Rodgers Chevrolet in Woodhaven, Michigan. Although, given very little she stayed diligent for decades, Pam took a failing location and turned it completely around. In the 2000's her dealership, *Rodgers Chevrolet*, was one of the most successful Chevrolet dealerships in the country. Before selling her dealership, her location was generating over $73 million dollars in annual revenue. She began with 25 employees and now boasts over 85; Rodgers Chevrolet received the Chevrolet Mark of Excellence award for outstanding sales every year since 2001. My cousin attributes her biggest hurdles as being rejected from the training program, the death of her first business partner, and battling the misconceptions of being a black woman in the industry.

"I am grateful for all my past experiences. The struggles in Flint and Flat Rock taught me survival skills that have sustained us through the last economic downturn."
Pamela Rodgers

She took the pain of rejection and turned it into one of the most successful car dealerships in the country. Once she locked in the vision of herself as one of the first female African-American dealers in the country, nothing but her level of focus would be the determining factor in connecting the vision to reality. One of my key takeaways from Cousin Pam's success is that she has always been a pioneer. In an industry dominated by men (especially in the 90's) she welcomed the challenge of being one of the first, despite the hurdles. She broke through a barrier, which is the key element in manifestation.

"The auto manufacturers did not want to take a chance on me and invest in a dealership opportunity. This became my inspiration - I was even more determined to become a dealer"
Pamela Rodgers

Dr. Eric Thomas

"My greatest asset is that I was homeless"
Dr. Eric Thomas

Speaking of the motor city, I would be remiss not to acknowledge one of the most inspirational speakers on the planet, Dr. Eric Thomas (ET). I began listening to ET in 2011 when I was working at the Verizon Wireless call center in Franklin, Tennessee. I happened to catch wind of his viral video of a young man enduring a vicious workout, preparing for an NFL tryout, while ET's voice over seemed to carry the young man through his grueling journey. On days when I was low, I would pull up ET's video, and watch it for the entirety of my shift. Since then I have followed ET, listening diligently to his uplifting messages, and shared his powerful videos with my students and friends. The meat and potatoes of ET's message is that he grew up without a father, raised by his mother in Detroit, Michigan. Like myself during that stage of life, ET saw little value in his academics and ultimately decided to drop out of high school. ET found himself homeless, sleeping in abandoned buildings, and eating out of trash cans. The turning point in his life came when a local Pastor spoke life into him. This Pastor saw Eric Thomas beyond his present circumstances, and helped Eric see new potential in his future. Today Eric Thomas travels the world, pouring that same message into anyone willing to listen. Many city centers of the Midwest have been drained economically. But buried inside of these areas commonly known as *"Legacy cities"* are some of the most resilient people you will find in the United States. ET is one of those individuals, and his message is timeless.

"Look at a man the way he is and he only becomes worse, but look at him as if he were what he could be, then he becomes what he should be"
Johann Wolfgang von Goethe

RON LEFLORE

Ron Leflore is an African American man who rose from the prison yard to the Major Leagues. I read about Leflore when I was 21, his story was in the timeless classic *Think & Grow Rich: A Black Choice*, by Napoleon Hill and Dennis Kimbro. Leflore was born and raised in Detroit, Michigan during the 1950's and 1960's. A city during that era was at the epicenter of racial tensions. Many African-Americans had migrated to northern cities like Cleveland and Detroit not only for economic opportunity, but to flee the racial terrorism they faced in the south. Ron had a difficult upbringing; his father was an unemployed alcoholic and his mother had to work significant hours to keep the family afloat. Some poor life decisions led Leflore to a prison cell in his early 20's, and he was ultimately delivered a 5-15-year sentence for armed robbery. While incarcerated, Ron played in the prison baseball league, and it became obvious he was head and shoulders above the other inmates. A fellow inmate convinced Billy Martin a manager for the Detroit Tigers to come observe Ron. After the observation Leflore was invited to a tryout at Tiger Stadium, and the rest is history. Ron Leflore played in the Major Leagues from 1974-1982 ending his career with the Chicago White Sox. There is a movie chronicling the life of Ron Leflore entitled, *One in a Million.* Although physically in bondage, he refused to wallow in despair, Ron was strength training, playing competitive baseball, and perfecting his craft with every crucial swing of the baseball bat. Ron was working and preparing for an opportunity he didn't know existed. Leflore literally went from a cold prison cell to a field of dreams, playing a kid's game for millions of dollars. What treasures are you sitting on? What dreams have you placed on hold, waiting for the right opportunity to present itself? The key to Ron Leflore' success was his ability to stay engaged while encaged.

"Adversity introduces a man to himself"

Albert Einstein

"An opportunity a man is unprepared for will only make him look foolish when it comes"

Napoleon Hill

CHAPTER II
IMAGINATION

"When I started out, I knew where I wanted to go and what I had to do

to get there. I painted a vivid picture in my mind of all the goals I

wanted to accomplish and simply set about the task of achieving them

one by one"

Walter Payton

Walter Payton is one the greatest running backs in NFL history. I remember reading about Walter Payton in my favorite book Think & Grow Rich: A Black Choice. The book went into detail about how Walter Payton understood the immense power of imagination. Before winning the with the 1986 Super bowl with the Chicago Bears, he imagined with great clarity all aspects of the post-game celebration. He could tell you the color of a fan's jacket deep into the stands. I was in awe but such detailed vision. He had envisioned every detail of his moment, well beyond just holding up the trophy. For a running back, vision is everything. Being able to predict a defenders angle of attack, react, accelerate, stop on a dime, cutback, juke, spin, run through a defender, and sometimes jump over a defender, all while holding onto the football are a few of the many characteristics that make a great running back. Walter Payton had all the physical tools, but also possessed something between his ears that allowed him to become legendary, his imagination. For the boy who grew up in humble beginnings in Columbia, Mississippi, raised by a father who was a factory worker, born in 1954 during the precipice of the Civil Rights movement, it is not hard to see where he honed his imaginative power. Walter Payton's imagination should be a blueprint for us all, how we too should be exercising our imaginations, and unlocking this transformative power.

CHAPTER III
LeBron James

"I see a young boy, he is sitting on a stoop in front of a vermin-infested
apartment house in Harlem. The stench of garbage is in the halls. The
drunks, the jobless, the junkies are shadow figures of his everyday
world"

Rev. Dr. Martin Luther King. Jr

"In the projects, you know it's hard times you see everything,
crackheads to drug dealers to gunshots every night to police sirens, and
I think it just made me stronger"

LeBron James

Grandma Clark despised when I hooked up my Sega Genesis to our 27-inch fatback Zenith television that sat on an old wooden TV stand in our small living room area, "Now ShoMari stop hooking that thang up, you gon mess up my picture." I thought she was selling wolf tickets, but in 2002, the picture on our Zenith actually played out, just as she prophesied. We resorted to a 9-inch black and white TV we had as a spare. This TV was so small yet had an infinitely long antenna wrapped in foil; the picture was blurry, snowy, and fuzzy. The tiny tube only picked up six channels, 2-7-16-22-45, and 64. As much as we were in love with the LeBron story, our circumstances wouldn't allow us to afford cable television, or a new television, but lucky for us all of the Cleveland Cavalier games broadcasted locally on Channel 64. Channel 64 was the fuzziest of the 6 channels we could get, but when we got it just right, we could see the game just fine. LeBron's size, headband, and swagger helped us distinguish him from the other players on the roster like Darius Miles, Carlos Boozer, and Ricky Davis. Grandma and I shared an instant love for LeBron. She was a surprisingly knowledgeable sports fan, considering we never had cable TV (I'm sure she gathered most of her information from the Dayton Daily Newspaper, she never threw away a paper). I was a sophomore in high school when the Cleveland Cavaliers drafted LeBron James, and Grandma and I vowed to never miss a game. The summer after he was drafted, I was scrambling to get to anyone's house who subscribed to NBA League Pass. I watched a few of LeBron's summer league games and would report back highlights to Grandma. "Did he win" she would ask, "Yes Grandma and he had two nasty dunks," I responded, she would then always say, "I just love LeBron he is such a good person." He was so inspiring to us, an Ohioan who rose from humble beginnings, and faced with insurmountable odds, in our mind he was just like us, or what we could be. We would sit on the same decrepit couch that doubled as her bed and watch LeBron make no-look passes, acrobatic chase-down blocks, jaw-dropping crossovers, and breaktaking dunks. I still remember how excited we would get watching LeBron catapult into the air for his signature one handed dunk, our intense celebrations would oftentimes cause us to lose the picture we worked so meticulously to secure. "Grandma stop jumping up and down," I'd say jokingly, then frantically sprint to the antenna and adjust until we got back to at least 50% visibility. These were some of my favorite times with Grandma, sitting on the floor, stomach rumbling, watching LeBron James rookie season on Channel 64.

I remained a huge LeBron fan during his successful run with the Miami Heat, while other Ohioans live streamed the sacrificial burning of their LeBron paraphernalia. I opted to hang my LeBron Cavs jerseys, save my ticket stubs from Cleveland games, and remained optimistic that he would return to the Cavs as soon as his contract allowed. I remember telling my despondent fellow Ohioans, "He's coming back." In 2012 I watched my childhood hero achieve his dream of becoming an NBA champion and I was elated. But I could tell something was missing from the King. LeBron had unfinished business in his hometown, with his community, and most importantly with himself. I was more convinced than ever he was coming home as soon as his contract allowed.

"I got a goal and that's a huge goal and that's to bring an NBA championship here to Cleveland and I won't stop until I get it"

LeBron James, Pre-Decision

My apartment in Bowling Green, Kentucky. 2010

I'M COMING HOME

In 2012 I was at a crossroads in life. I was living in Nashville, Tennessee on my own and loved the experience of surviving in the big city, but I wasn't making enough money to sustain. I was one flat tire or overheating radiator from being up shits creek. Every day before making the drive from my apartment complex on Nolensville and Thompson Lane out to the suburbs in Franklin, TN, I would say at least three prayers for the sake of my 2001 Chevrolet Impala. I just knew one day soon my engine would quit acknowledging the fact that I was entering the key and turning it clockwise, and then I would lose my job at Verizon Wireless, and be back at square one. On top of that, I hated my job, and I just felt like I could be doing something more impactful with my degree. One day after a frustrated shift I picked up the phone and called my good friend Torrey back home in Dayton, "Aye bra I'm really struggling down here, you got an open room?" He immediately welcomed me with open arms, "Of course bra bra, mi casa, su casa," he said with a brotherly tone that can only be built through decades of struggle. In August 2012 I uprooted my life in Nashville and relocated to Torrey's spare room in Bellbrook, Ohio a suburb of Dayton. After returning home from college I attempted to chase my dream of becoming a personal trainer, but I was in no financial position to support the dream of becoming my own boss, most days I was excited if I could scrape up enough change for a $5 footlong from Subway. So, I took a few odd jobs, hoping to save up enough money to pursue my dream of owning my own gym. Upon relocating to Ohio, I immediately found a job for $24,000/year working for Obama's re-election campaign *Organizing for America*. This job required me to get Dayton residents registered to vote, aka get as many signatures as I could on these voter registration forms. I knocked on doors, made thousands of calls, and hung outside liquor stores hoping to garner enough daily signatures to keep my word of $300 monthly rent to Torrey. I remember one night my co-workers and I were required to sleep outside in tents in the middle of a storm to raise awareness for the *Get Out The Vote* campaign. After this night I knew that working with politically charged college students wasn't my cup of tea. My next gig was working as a sales associate/trainer/janitor for Premiere Fitness in Centerville, Ohio. This job was odd because my manager, who told us to call him "Snake" told me that I needed to sign up for a membership in order to work out there, even though I was an employee. I reluctantly signed the suspicious pink contract, but after talking to a few of my cousins who were getting their wages garnished by this very gym, I cancelled my

170

contract and employment with the company. Next was a gig working at the newly built Dick's Sporting Goods in the Dayton Mall, this job required that I help put together the store but was made no guarantee of employment after the store was complete. My spree of odd jobs culminated in 2014 when I was hired as a *Specialist* for the new Apple Store opening in Beavercreek, Ohio. It was July 11, 2014, and I was in the lobby of Hampton Inn, Beavercreek, Ohio. There was something very eerie about that day, and I remember walking into the hotel lobby where I saw sports journalist Brian Windhorst speaking on one of the TV's with a Cleveland Cavaliers background behind him. LeBron made a decision that shook up the entire sports world. Born and raised in Ohio like LeBron I always felt a parallel connection to his journey. We both grew up poor, in Ohio, without a father present in the home, and our mothers even share the same name, Gloria. When LeBron made the decision to return to Ohio, it was a confidence booster for me. Here was this global icon, one of my childhood inspirations, who can play basketball for any team in the NBA, but he chose to come back to the Midwest, to the Rustbelt, back home.

As an executive producer, LeBron has highlighted injustices in amateur athletics, speaks out against racial discrimination, and has provided a platform for athletes to discuss a plethora of important issues in our society. LeBron opened the I Promise school in 2018 to support at-risk students and their parents in the Akron, Ohio area. This school seeks to provide support for kids that might slip through the cracks and fall victim to the system. This is an example of educating the whole child. They have not only addressed the curriculum, but the outside needs of these children and their parents. As an educator and student who grew up in an abusive environment, I know the issues these students face all too well. Students are not mentally available to learn until we address the needs of safety, hunger, and transportation. LeBron James stands next to Muhammad Ali as a sports icon who uses his platform as a voice for the black race.

Despite all my vertical jump training, and knowledge of exercise science, I did not become a professional athlete like Bron', but I attribute sizable credit to LeBron James for inspiring me to overcome my particular bout with oppressive poverty. LeBron used the pain of poverty and the absence of a father to push him into becoming an amazing husband, father, and humanitarian. Thank you, LeBron, for being a role model, trailblazer, and inspiration to an entire generation, and thank you for bringing one of the dopest parades in sports history right down Euclid avenue. You inspired my Grandmother and I when everything around us was crumbling and you continue to inspire us to this day.

"Cleveland this is for you"
LeBron James

I Promise School - Akron, Ohio

The Akronite

Scripted against a backboard of broken dreams,
Dry red and gold paint, Wooden floors Broken hearts
A shattered team,
Another season signed off in Cleveland left Flooded again with cold
blooded losses the echoes of Empty Nets...
Yet Written in the stars
A hero will rise up again
Bring a legendary story
Glory back to the Midwest
This time Redemption will come back to the land
A championship Will come to the Q
All of it due to the Summit man his band of brothers
Putting in work and game tight
Doubling up in the gym
A hundred miles of tape runnin'
Getting the game right to be a Champ it will take more Blood,
Take more sweat
It will take faith over fate strength over pain, pain over fear
It will take new Ways to chase the imperial throne switching up
weapons of battle
Stepping out of the comfort Zone
take A village to persevere, Take a city, A Family to hold him down
A mother's love on the sidelines holding her sons crown
Yelling go get em baby let em know
Glow under pressure show these children
This ain't given you earn the right to be here
The right to be their hero, the iron lion, da ga gan of the of 3.3.0
get em 'Bron do it for the land
Be mighty in your clutch Humble in your stand, Stand dominant in the
paint magnificent in the lane
Stay opulent in your fight legendary in your flight
Stay classic in your one-legged leap to the rim
All hail King James
All hail to the Akronite All hail to the leader who Stood up to his role

173

Who bounced back with his state his mind his body and His Rubber City Soul.
Lemon Andersen
#JustAKidFromAkron

CHAPTER IV
The Law of Attraction

I love data, I believe data is important for providing context, but never for one moment allow data to define your potential. Economist, nutritionist, education analyst and every other statistician that once predicted my future must adjust my dot up or down their respective scatter plot. My adverse childhood environment has left me with the gift of stamina. A stamina that refuses to quit, despite the improbable likelihood of my desired outcome. I believe that I am the architect of this particular existence. I believe in my power to bend reality, and so should you. You have the power within you to endure, to change, to grow, and to become. It is our responsibility to remain steadfast in the process of creation and manifestation. We must stay true to our principles in the midst of uncertainty and learn to endure during tumultuous spells of silence. Understanding that the process of manifestation is not on our watch, but to the degree we maximize our resources, talents, time. Through this effort, our ability to collapse time is potentiated. During those times it seems as if the universe has forsaken us we must work even harder towards our goals. This is the metaphor of Jesus dying on the cross during His last few earthly moments. God had not forsaken Jesus, but in this time of pain and agony Jesus was unclear of the universal intentions for His destiny. We are never forsaken, as long as we have breath in our lungs, we have the ability to make adjustments to our lives and redirect our course.

"My God, my God, why have you forsaken me?"
Matthew 27:46.

174

Meet the Parents

"I'm used to not having a lot, I'm from the gutter"

Jay-Z - Best of Me

I am not your typical millennial. I am not the culmination of Saturday morning football practices, trips to Disney world, and piano recitals. In my apartment you won't find many trophies or medals commemorating priceless childhood moments, just painful memories from the sideline, watching others live out their childhood. As a youth, I couldn't quite articulate my struggle, or define my war, I only knew that I was fighting one. I wasn't quite sure what year it started, or what led to it being fought in the first place, only that it weighed on me like a barbell that was too heavy to even lift off the bench. I knew that my enemy was clever, relentless, a chameleon, and her only aim was to oppress my potential. I didn't know that when my father decided to walk away from his brown skin prince, that he named ShoMari, which is Swahili for strong warrior, that he was altering more than just the microeconomics of my existence. But if Dad was Richard Nixon, launching my war, then Gloria was Bill Clinton, as her policies were more discreet, yet far more devastating to my future. She established a private prison at Grandmas estate, in which she was the warden, and I the star inmate. She developed policies and rules that sophisticatedly governed my everyday world. She calculated my improbable statistical survival by factoring in my "worse in state" high-poverty school district, prevalent police presence, a rat-infested home, economic scarcity, and the streets themselves. She knew I'd be swallowed up one way or another, but her ace in the hole was my psyche itself. The physical prison was torture, but the mental one was damnation. Staring at my backpack for the next roach to crawl out, instead of focusing on the chalkboard, dreaming of a bed instead of an ivy league scholarship, this was an ingenious, masterful technique, a Molotov cocktail of Ronald Reagan and Willie Lynch. She not only controlled my physical freedom, she sought to destroy my ability to dream. Gloria designed my circumstances in a way that all I ever saw was darkness, and that I only felt oppression. We have never hugged, never looked one another in the eye, and never said I love you. When I explain this to friends, or past girlfriends it always strikes them as odd, and largely unbelievable, but it is fact. I never agreed with my upbringing, nor did I sign up for such circumstances. I would have preferred a two-parent home, a prestigious high school where I could have fed my thirst for knowledge and maximized my academic potential. But that was not my path, and this book would not be so if not for those challenges. My cousin Kendra recently told me something that I must include in this final chapter, "Sometimes we must forgive our parents, they also have childhoods they need to recover from." Following her charge, I began to reflect on my parent's upbringing, and I was able to see how some of their childhood pains manifested as adults and as parents.

Dad spent portions of his childhood overseas, he was moved from school to school due to Grandpas military obligations. He knows not one person from his childhood who he can call a friend. I did some research on military brats and found that this particular population especially during the 1950-1970's indeed has a higher rate of divorce and possess many other symptoms that my dad exudes. All rooted in knowing that he would not be at one place for too long before having to pick up and move again. Learning never to get too attached to a particular school, favorite teacher, childhood friend, or significant other, because soon you would be moving and would most likely never see that person again. This information helped me understand why it was so easy for him to leave me, and my siblings.

Gloria never exuded the traits that I thought came naturally to all mothers. I thought about the hoarding, the lack of genuine love and affection, and could only find a correlation to what Dr. Joy DeGruy refers to as, "Post Traumatic Slave Syndrome." By this she means, multi-generational trauma that is passed down through our DNA. A trauma that began on the western shores of Africa with capture and selling of my ancestors, and continued throughout their inhumane treatment on Southern plantations. I imagine someone in my lineage was sold away from their mother, and that mother's way of coping with such a horrific experience was to emotionally detach herself from that child, the same emotional detachment that exists between Gloria and me. As I mentioned in ACT I, Grandma Clark also possesses hoarding tendencies, which are rooted in her own humble beginnings in Munford, Alabama. Grandma never wanted to throw away anything because she never had anything. I do not agree with how I was raised, or the challenges I endured, but I have learned to forgive, understanding that hurt individuals carry hurt with them, and I want to provide the best possible environment of growth for my future children.

"I didn't write this book because I've accomplished something extraordinary, I wrote this book because I've achieved something quite ordinary which doesn't happen to most kids that grow up like me"

J.D Vance - Hillbilly Elegy

CHAPTER V
WKU

"One day during my senior year, my eyes were opened, and I never

viewed my captivity the same"

ShoMari Payne - Buckeye Nights

As a boy my picture of the world was viewed through the narrow lens of my oppressive poverty. In my mind formal education possessed no power to change my environment or present circumstances, so I quit putting forth effort, and largely quit going to school altogether. In grade school I realized that no matter how well I read, how precocious my inquisitions, or how accurately I spelled, I would still be confined to sleep on the floor that night. School was powerless in transforming my immediate needs, and I only valued the power and sacrifice of education when it manifested itself into a tangible opportunity. The day education became powerful in my mind was a rainy October day during my senior year of high school. This happened to be one of the 67 days I actually went to school that year. My classmates and I were pulled out of Ms. Cook's English class and into the school library. We were all pretty upset about it, I knew damn well I couldn't get into any University with my GPA, but reluctantly all 40 or so of us sat down to hear from a couple of college recruiters.

The college was Western Kentucky University (WKU), I had never heard of it. There were two recruiters, both white, one a skinny male with dark brown hair, and the other an equally skinny female with long brown hair. They seemed a little nervous initially, maybe because of their nearly all black audience. I remember a couple girls started doing another girls hair right before the presentation. The presenters began their pitch and went into detail describing WKU and how awesome it was, like all the other recruiters did about their schools. They passed out these red pamphlets and began telling us about the admissions requirements. I flipped open the pamphlet and immediately became intrigued by the dining options, I was fascinated that they had a Pizza

Hut and Chic-fil-A on campus. Nonetheless, this is where I would usually tune out, distract the presenter, or start making jokes, but for some reason I was all ears. "So the great thing about WKU is that we have two ways to gain admission, either a 2.5 GPA, or a 20 on the ACT exam," the female recruiter with excitement in her tone. I immediately raised my hand, "So if you have below a 2.5 you can still get in as long as you get a 20 on the ACT," I asked. "Good question, that's absolutely right, it doesn't matter your GPA if you score a 20 or above your granted full admission," the young man responded. After the presentation I snuck off and caught up with the recruiters before they reached the metal detectors on their way to the parking lot. I just kept it straight with them, "I have like a 1.0 GPA, but your saying I can still get admitted if I get a 20 ACT?" The guy seemed a little puzzled to hear such low a number for a GPA, he consulted with his colleague for a second and said, "Yea that's our policy, good luck on the ACT, we would love to have you on the Hill if you can get the score."

First-time Freshmen Requirements

Students must meet ONE of the following requirements for admission.

1. ACT composite of 20 or greater, or
2. SAT combined score of 1020 or greater (940 or greater combined score accepted for tests taken prior to March, 2016)*, or
3. Unweighted high school GPA of 2.50 or higher, or
4. Achieve the required Composite Admission Index (CAI) score

WKU Admission Requirements

Western Kentucky University's admissions policy was not intended for students like me. It was probably not the University's intention to have the campus flooded with low-performing students from the inner-city. In 2004 WKU was on the rise, and the University implemented a strategy to compete with middle of the road institutions in surrounding states. They were the beneficiary of a talented young hoop star named Courtney Lee (New York Knicks) from Indianapolis, Indiana, who put the basketball program on the map leading the team to back-to-back sweet sixteen appearances. WKU had recently won the 2002 NCAA D1AA football championship, bringing their football program to national prominence, which helped solidify the jump to Division 1 football. What WKU needed to support this new growth strategy was students, otherwise known as tuition dollars. WKU was widely considered the third best public institution in the state, behind the University of Kentucky, and the University of Louisville, so the strategy for increasing enrollment was to look beyond the bluegrass state for numbers, and heavily recruit students from surrounding states. But why would students from Ohio, Kentucky, Indiana, who were not going to be collegiate athletes choose WKU over their own middle of the road, in-state institutions? To combat this challenge WKU implemented a tuition reduction program called the "Tuition Incentive Program", which offers discounted tuition to students who reside in select counties in neighboring states, one county being my very own Montgomery County of Ohio. These factors helped transform WKU from a small, in-state University, to a melting pot of diversity, and an increased undergraduate enrollment upwards of 20,000 students. Despite this strategy for growth, WKU's unique admission policy was still not meant for students like me, I was certainly an outlier, a loophole in a policy meant for students within close reach of the desired 2.5 GPA. Their policy was intended for a young girl from Evansville, Indiana with a 2.3 GPA due to her marching band and cheerleading commitments. The policy was meant for a WKU legacy student holding a 2.0 GPA, whose parents would be devastated if their child was denied admission into their beloved alma mater. But for me? An African-American boy who quit taking academics serious around the 3rd or 4th grade, that was sitting at a 1.2 cumulative GPA? A boy that may very well bring a fleet of roaches to campus and require a costly dormitory fumigation? I was certainly the exception, not the rule. When the two young WKU representatives pulled up to Jefferson High School in the sticks of Dayton, Ohio and spoke to a room full of black seniors, I'm sure they didn't think much would manifest from that particular trip. When they pulled into our school parking lot I wonder if they contemplated turning around when they saw the metal detectors, or how long they sat in their Dodge Neon smoking cigarettes in frustration before they entered. Ultimately none of that matters, because they had no choice but to come in, and I had no choice but to be at school and in their presentation. The secret with energy that is so critical to everything in this book is this, **I MANIFESTED THEIR TRIP**. My pain reservoir had runneth over, my universal pleas had been heard, and my desire for a new life had been answered with a tangible reality. It is almost spooky, but nothing else has ever made more logical sense. A boy whose home was frequently visited by the police for being truant, had no reason to be in school on that particular day. A boy whose long behavioral record usually suggested to school administrators that I need not be part of such important college admission presentations was allowed to participate. A boy who usually would be searching for an opportunity to frustrate the presenters through comedy was fully attentive. I had been told majority of my life that I would NEVER do anything of significance. And in school that message was even more clear than it was from the roaches and rats at home.

My high school counselor grew tired of my questions regarding potential scenarios in which I might still graduate. "What if I do Geometry on correspondence, and do junior English during summer school," I'd ask, "You're going to be here five years at minimum," he'd respond. But when WKU passed out those crisp red admission packets, it was truly love at first sight, and I was determined to graduate on time. To this very day I can still remember the smell of the pamphlets, it must have been the same smell in the air on January 31, 1865 when Lincoln approved the joint Resolution of Congress to abolish slavery. Or the same smell when I first visited WKU for orientation, or the smell of my Grandpa Payne's closet, it smelled like all of those things. After the admission reps from WKU visited my high school and explained their admission policy, I immediately envisioned myself living on campus. I frequently found myself exploring www.wku.edu, studying the campus map, fantasizing over which dormitory I would reside, and pictured myself dining at the campus restaurants. In my mind I was completely immersed in the culture, making friends, working out at the Rec center, and sleeping like a newborn baby on my very own twin size bed in the dormitory. Those two angels from WKU stretched me, beyond anything I had ever dreamed possible. This stretching was coupled with physical power through my newfound belief. This was how Orville and Wilbur must have felt when they completed the first successful flight in history for 12 seconds and covered 120 feet. After their inaugural flight, they no longer entertained the critics, they had seen their dream come to fruition first-hand. Conversely, the roaches and clutter at my house in Dayton no longer affected me the same way, I had expanded my vision of myself. In that same hoarded home, I carved out a small space on the floor and began practicing for the ACT. The 20 on the ACT **OR** a 2.5 GPA gave me hope, it gave me something to strive for. I made the decision that there was a better life for me than the one I was given. There were no guarantees, I just felt for the first time in my life something was within my control. I couldn't go back to freshman year and repair my GPA, but I could prepare for a standardized test. I carved out a small place to sit in one of the hoarded bedrooms and began studying diligently for the ACT. I remember mice running across the bedroom, and roaches crawling up the walls, but I did my best to sit there, back pressed against rubber maids, shoe boxes, and wired hangers, and to lock in on studying.

Where I studied for the ACT

The Perfect Storm

I took the ACT on a cold rainy Saturday December 11, 2004. I caught the bus downtown Dayton to the private Chaminade Julienne high school, and remember thinking, damn this school is nice. I saw students being dropped off by their parents, tight hugs, big kisses, and well wishes being passed across the parking lot. I sat outside for a moment before entering the school, and remember thinking to myself, "Nigga there is no way you are going to score a 20 on this test, you have the worst GPA at your school." I contemplated just hopping back on the bus and trying to figure out another strategy for getting out from under

184

Gloria's system, but I ultimately decided to take the test, and the rest is history.

Test	Description	Score	Date	Expiration Date
A01	ACT English	19	01-DEC-2004	
A02	ACT Math	16	01-DEC-2004	
A03	ACT Reading	23	01-DEC-2004	
A04	ACT Science Reasoning	20	01-DEC-2004	
A05	ACT Composite	20	01-DEC-2004	

Results from the ACT

Batman: "You told me a child did it"

Old Man: "But no ordinary child, a child born in hell, forged from suffering, hardened by pain, not a man from privilege"

Dark Knight Rises

Pain is a Stimulus

Office of Admissions
270-745-2551
FAX: 270-745-6133
admission@wku.edu

WESTERN
KENTUCKY
UNIVERSITY

Western Kentucky University
1 Big Red Way
Bowling Green, KY 42101-3576

January 24 2005

Shomari Nkosi Payne
1550 Kimmel Ln
Dayton, OH   45418

Dear Shomari:

Congratulations! You have been admitted to Western Kentucky University.

The Admissions Committee has carefully reviewed your file and is confident Western will benefit from your addition to our community. We also feel you will benefit from the rich history and tradition of our university.

Your admission is tentative until your file is complete. The Office of Admissions will require final transcripts from any previous educational institution you have attended prior to enrolling at Western Kentucky University. If any other documents are incomplete, you should arrange for final academic records to be sent to us as soon as possible. You will not be permitted to register for a second term until your admissions file is complete.

If you have not had the opportunity, I would like to personally invite you to visit campus. During your visit you may tour the campus, meet with an admissions counselor, visit with a faculty member, and talk with current Western students. I'm sure you will be impressed by the many opportunities available at Western as well as the friendly atmosphere of the campus. In addition, be confident that as a Western student you will have the commitment of every faculty and staff member to provide you with the best possible educational experience.

Enclosed you will find your admission profile. Please review your profile to ensure that the information is complete and accurate. To update information, record corrections to the right of the information listed and return the profile to the Office of Admissions. If you prefer, you may notify us of corrections via e-mail using the address listed above.

Welcome to the Hill!

Hilltopper

"God shuffled the cards, dealt me a hand with impossible odds, put an
obstacle course up, look and I conquered em all"
J.Cole - Tribe

I decided to leave my oppressive environment in Dayton and open my mind to something different, an entirely new galaxy as far as I was concerned. I was 17 years old, with no plan, no support, no tangible skills, no resources, and no scholarship. I knew no one else that was going to WKU and I had no family in the area. The only thing that I was 100% sure of was that the way to a better life was somewhere far from where I grew up, far from the roaches, miles from the mice. I imagined having a meal plan and never going to bed hungry again, with my choice from the plethora of campus restaurants only a short walk away. Although for the moment my circumstances were still the same, I had finally activated a crucial piece of my existence, my vision and imagination. The universe provided a way, and when my opportunity presented itself, I capitalized. As I reflect on this miracle, the odds are truly astronomical.

CHAPTER VI
Manifestation

"Only when standing at the brink of destruction does man truly realize
his potential"
Ancient Samurai Maxim

The secret to manifestation is clarity and intention. I did not have a laundry list of college options like most high school students, you know the ones who sit down at dinner tables with their parents and together develop their list of potential schools, weighing pro's and con's, researching esteemed alumni, and the credentials of the Faculty members. I did not tour the countryside and receive persuasive pitches, nor was I awarded a healthy scholarship package. Manifestation demands our full commitment, and from grade school onwards I was not a committed student. But as I stated in ACT I, I prayed to God for seventeen years for an upgrade to my life. From the time I became conscious of my circumstances, I was constantly asking God to deliver me from them. The consistency of those prayers was cosmically unignorable. It is the law of nature, Reap and Sow, Ask and Receive, Seek and you shall Find.

"Your testimony is the key that can unlock someone's prison"

Lady Ardys Leslie

Europe

"They have greatly oppressed me from my youth, but they have not

gained the victory over me."

Psalms 129:2

Something unbelievable happened to me last summer. I was given the opportunity to explore Europe for a month. Many nights I scroll through my iPhone photos in awe that I was able to immerse myself in different cultures, explore ancient artifacts, and truly expand my horizons. I caught a boat ride across the Seine River in Paris and snapped over 100 photos of the Eiffel Tower. I soaked in all the breathtaking portraits in the Louvre and took countless selfies with Mona Lisa. I laughed with Uber drivers who hailed from all across the globe and could feel the genuineness in their tone when they told me to have fun and be safe. I was mesmerized by the architecture of the Sagrada Família in Barcelona and enjoyed exquisite seafood at El Cangrejo while starting out across the Mediterranean Sea. I watched for hours while locals played the drums at the Puerta del Sol square in Madrid and spent hours in one of the largest libraries in the world, the Museo de la Biblioteca Nacional. I stood in astonishment looking out across the Roman Coliseum, thinking about all the pain that occurred in the ancient stadium. I stood with what felt like a thousand people in silence as we soaked in the vastness of the Sistine Chapel in the Vatican. I window shopped in Firenze, Italy, saw the famous *David* statue by Michelangelo, and ate Gelato for the first time. I felt a heaviness in my heart while walking through the Memorial to the Murdered Jews of Europe in Berlin, and a parallel heaviness as I traced the steps of imprisoned Jews at the Sachsenhausen Concentration Camp in Oranienburg, Germany. I explored the vast collection of Ancient Egyptian artifacts in the British Museum in London and caught JAY-Z and Beyoncé's *On the Run II* concert in London Stadium, just by pure happenstance (first concert ever). This experience was the closing chapter to the first 30 years of my life. When I was seventeen, I could have never imagined leaving the country, let alone spending a month backpacking throughout Europe. My upbringing had never demanded such a vision for my life, I only wished for a bed to sleep in, no more hoarding, no more rats, and no more roaches. But the Universe had something else in mind, a better life was waiting for me, I only needed to activate the power that lived within me all along, the power of vision.

*"THAT WHAT YOU HOLD IN YOUR MIND LIKE A PRECIOUS
TREASURE WILL FIND ITSELF MANIFESTED IN THE UNIVERSE"*
ShoMari Payne

Still I Rise

You may write me down in history
With your bitter, twisted lies,
You may trod me in the very dirt
But still, like dust, I'll rise.

Does my sassiness upset you?
Why are you beset with gloom?
'Cause I walk like I've got oil wells
Pumping in my living room.

Just like moons and like suns,
With the certainty of tides,
Just like hopes springing high,
Still I'll rise.

Did you want to see me broken?
Bowed head and lowered eyes?
Shoulders falling down like teardrops.
Weakened by my soulful cries.

Does my haughtiness offend you?
Don't you take it awful hard

'Cause I laugh like I've got gold mines
Diggin' in my own backyard.

You may shoot me with your words,
You may cut me with your eyes,
You may kill me with your hatefulness,
But still, like air, I'll rise.

Does my sexiness upset you?
Does it come as a surprise
That I dance like I've got diamonds
At the meeting of my thighs?

Out of the huts of history's shame
I rise
Up from a past that's rooted in pain
I rise
I'm a black ocean, leaping and wide,
Welling and swelling I bear in the tide.
Leaving behind nights of terror and fear
I rise
Into a daybreak that's wondrously clear
I rise
Bringing the gifts that my ancestors gave,

I am the dream and the hope of the slave.

I rise

I rise

I rise.

Maya Angelou

Final Thoughts

One day I realized that my story is not about me, it is about every other child that hails from the ghetto. It's about those kids I taught in the inner-city who have the odds stacked against them. It's about those individuals growing up in disinvested communities who have subconsciously succumbed to the culture of violence, lawlessness, and displaced anger. It's about every person you have the potential to touch. Your story is not commonplace, and neither is theirs. After hiding this chapter of my life for majority of my existence something dawned on me, the revelation that this story does not belong to me, but to the universe. I am just the chosen warrior for this particular battle, and what I found on my journey was meant to illuminate a path for others to follow. I thank the roaches and rats, they taught me that the ground is no place for a champion. I thank my parents for their absence, they taught me how to survive on my own. I thank my Grandfather for all of his lessons, and only wish that I had embraced them sooner. I would like to dedicate this book to everyone who is discontent with their present circumstances. I poured my heart into these words and I pray that is a blessing and sparks the change you are seeking in your own life. As I said in the opening, writing this book has been my greatest accomplishment, and one of my fiercest challenges. Putting into words an experience that often brings me to tears was not easy. But at the front of my mind I thought about everyone that I could help through sharing my story. This was my experience navigating through poverty, lack, and oppression. I hope this book helps to strengthen the research on children growing up in oppressive poverty. This book was birthed with the intention of rewriting the narrative for the disadvantaged, and to apprehend the criminal of childhood potential. My prayer is that this book inspires you. I imagine 50 years from now a young African-American teen flipping through his audiobook collection, and after he listens to the Chronicles of King & X, followed by his adventures with Dr. Michael Eric Dyson and his workout powered by Dr. Eric Thomas, right after he is mesmerized by the infinite penmanship of Ta-Nahesi Coates, he presses play on my story, my contribution to the black community, and to the planet at large.

Pain is a Stimulus

Life handed me roaches, I turned it into a dissertation, life handed me poverty I turned it into motivation, life served me struggle, and I pray that it is your inspiration.

Thank you

Author's Acknowledgments and Citations

This book would not have been possible without the inspiration of authors, scientists, athletes, coaches, researchers, journalists, artists, poets, entrepreneurs, educators, and change agents who invest their lives into many of the topics discussed in this book. I would like to thank the Creator for life, consciousness, and health. God's timing is perfect. This is my story, but it does not belong solely to me, it is an American story of resilience. I am grateful that I was chosen as an ambassador for this unique struggle, and I pray that my story become a light to illuminate a path for those whom may need.

I would like to thank a few of my role models for their unbeknownst mentorship throughout my development. When I seek motivation, knowledge, and encouragement, I lean on your passion as my inspiration.

LeBron James, Michelle Alexander, Dr. Henry Louis Gates Jr., Eric Thomas, Inky Johnson, Ta-Nehisi Coates, Dennis Kimbro, Les Brown, Malcolm Gladwell, Nas, Jay-Z, J.Cole, Common, Paul Tough, Drew Philp, Dr.Ruby Payne, Dr. Nadine Harris, Richard Rothstein, Antonio Moore, Dr. Boyce Watkins, Meek Mill, Drake, Dr. Joe Dispenza, Brian Nunez, Dr. Richard Gates.

A special recognition to the heroes, mentors, and trailblazers that have physically transcended this life, yet through their sacrifice to humanity, fuel my daily journey.

Dr. Martin Luther King Jr., Coretta Scott King, W.E.B Dubois, Carter G Woodson, Harriet Tubman, Malcolm X, Kenneth B. Clark, Napoleon Hill, Tupac Shakur, Muhammad Ali, Langston Hughes, Raymond Holliwell, Howard Zinn, Dr. Ivan Van Sertima, Maya Angelou, Stephen Covey, Ralph Waldo Emerson, Albert Einstein, Alan Watts, Whitney Young, Thomas Dutton, Fred Hampton, Jane Jacobs, Ida B. Wells.

Special thanks to the friends/mentors/colleagues that I've had the gracious pleasure of encountering thus far along my journey.

Patricia Peters, Melissa Ward, Tad Frei, Corinne Patterson, Derrick Jenkins, Sarah Acton, Sue Kowalski, Ron Hunter, Sharon Hunter LaDawn Mims, Bryan Dell, Vincent Gonzales, Coach Mayfield, Coach Steed, Marti Kyger, Jim Stearns, Monique Frost, Emma Robertson, Debbie Coleman, Emily Akil, Michelle Thomas, Diana Peterson.

Thank You To all of my family members

Camille Payne, Aunt Mildred, Avery Payne, Jaelyn Payne,
Chris Dixon, LaKisha Payne, Jaron Payne, Micah Payne,
Aunt Cynthia, Ali Payne, LaShonda Payne, Karma Payne,
Uncle Art, Aunt Nancy, Aunt Rita, Aunt Donna, Uncle Barry,
India Beavers, Rhylie Hogue, Bryant Keeble.Jr, Jada Beavers,
Britany Keeble, Kendra Martin-Towles, Chris Scurry, Whitney
Manson, Dorothy Thomas, Shanelle Martin, DeQuita Means,
Wade Flemming.

**To all my childhood and adulthood friends that have become family, thank you for the love, support, encouragement, hospitality, and loyalty.
I would like to Thank You**

Torrey Parker, Anthony Marsh III, Kevin McAdoo, Jasmine
Johnson, Leshea Orr, Carl Moore, Nate Cole, Shawn Stewart,
Stephen Bivens, Graham Williamson, Derrick Moss,
Alandre Tidwell, Lamar Alston, Nicholas Hicks, Austin Hicks,
William "Bear" Lowery, Austin Hicks, Chaz Jones,
DeShawn Harris, Chris Mobley, Michael Walters, Joshua Nalls,
Cassius Bell, Mario Drake, Marques Parker.

Thank you to the parents in my community who opened your doors, spare-rooms, pocket-books, futons, couches, and refrigerators to a young boy who needed every bit of your love. You said yes, when you had every reason to say no, I never forgot, and I thank you for your sacrifices.

Ms. Karen Lewis, Mrs.Vance, Ms. Debra Woodard,

Mr. Anthony Marsh II & Mrs. Renise Marsh, Mrs. Walters,

Ms. Lesha Orr, Ms. Robin Mobley, Mr. Dan Arnold,

Mr. Lamar Drake & Mrs. Yvonne Drake, Ms. Twila Lewis-White,

Mr. Tony & Mrs. Jameka Parker.

Thank you to all of my students at Dayton Public Schools, Sinclair Community College, and Miami University for teaching me so much through our interactions. You all were the driving force in allowing me to finish this work.

Special Thank You

Grandma Alice Clark, thank you for accepting the task of raising me as your son. Although we had little, your love and sacrifice were the driving force in my childhood. You are my angel now and forever.

Grandpa Curtis W. Payne Sr., I have never known another love like yours. Thank you for seventeen amazing years of laughs, joy, wisdom, hugs, lectures, pancakes, sermons, and backyard lessons. You are my hero and I reflect on your love every day. Rest peacefully King.

Rest in Peace

Papa Clark

Aunt Louise

Grannie Payne

Grandpa Payne

Lynn Montgomery

LeRoy Martin

Wilhelmina Flemming

Willie Flemming

NOTES

1.   Department of Commerce, *Money Income and Poverty Status in the United States: 1987.* https://www2.census.gov/library/publications/1988/demographics/p60-161.pdf

2.   *Compulsive hoarding: current controversies and new directions.* Centers for Disease Control and Prevention, 2010. https://www.ncbi.nlm.nih.gov/pubmed/12281534

3.   Ronald Takaki, A Different Mirror; *A History of Multicultural America.* 1993.

4.   Metropolitan Boston Housing Partnership, *Rethinking Hoarding Intervention.* 2015 http://www.philadelphiahoarding.org/resources/MBHP-Hoarding-Report-2015_FINAL.pdf

5.   Michelle Alexander, *The New Jim Crow.* 2012

6.   Sara Solovitch - *Hoarding is a serious disorder — and it's only getting worse in the U.S.*- Washington Post. 2016 https://www.washingtonpost.com/national/health-science/hoarding-is-serious-disorder--and-its-only-getting-worse-in-the-us/2016/04/11/b64a0790-f689-11e5-9804-537defcc3cf6_story.html?utm_term=.07fe0635999f

7.   Jay McDonald, *Professor Randy Frost: 'Merely clearing things out' Doesn't fix hoarding.* 2014. https://www.sparefoot.com/self-storage/blog/6790-interview-with-randy-frost-about-hoarding/

8. Ta-Nahesi Coates, *The Case for Reparations*. 2014 https://www.theatlantic.com/magazine/archive/2014/06/the-case-for-reparations/361631/

9. Brian Doucet, *Inner Cities, Inner Suburbs, Outer Suburbs: geographies, changing preferences.* 2010 http://www.geographyjobs.com/articles/inner_cities_inner_suburbs_ou ter_suburbs_geographies_changing_preferences.html

10. Justin Charity, *What Does "Inner City" Mean, Anyway?* 2016 https://www.complex.com/life/2016/02/inner-city-origin-and-proliferation-of-sloppy-political-language

11. Samuel R. Staley. *Dayton, Ohio: The Rise, Fall and Stagnation of a Former Industrial Juggernaut.* New Geography, 2008. http://www.newgeography.com/content/00153-dayton-ohio-the-rise-fall-and-stagnation-a-former-industrial-juggernaut

12. Badger, Miller, Pearce and Quealy, *Extensive Data Shows Punishing Reach of Racism for Black Boys.* 2018 https://www.nytimes.com/interactive/2018/03/19/upshot/race-class-white-and-black-men.html

13. Napoleon Hill, Dennis Kimbro. *Think & Grow Rich: A Black Choice,* 2011.

14. Dr. Nadine Harris, *How childhood trauma affects across a lifetime.* TEDMED. 2014. https://www.ted.com/talks/nadine_burke_harris_how_childhood_trau ma_affects_health_across_a_lifetime

15. Joe Gurnig, *Dayton area named on list of most segregated regions.*
     Dayton Daily News. 2017.
     http://www.mydaytondailynews.com/news/dayton-area-named-list-
     most-segregated-
     regions/kOLCijJunxGzeS7kP2rKyL/?ecmp=daytondaily_social_faceb
     ook_2014_s

16. Jeremy P. Kelly. *Trotwood, Jefferson each have a "worst in state"*
     score. Dayton Daily News. 2017.
     http://www.daytondailynews.com/news/trotwood-jefferson-each-have-
     worst-state-score/GFwl7J1XnezdH7ZJKpogIP/

17. Terry Morris. *Air Force to bid last farewell to DESC.* Dayton Daily
     News. 2013.
     http://www.daytondailynews.com/news/local/air-force-bid-last-
     farewell-desc/3b3qvKHMInAq9YITO7UcAN/

18. WHIOTV. *Suspect indicted after man found dead in car.* 2017.
     https://www.whio.com/news/breaking-news/suspect-indicted-after-
     dayton-man-found-dead-car/cIC3VBoQ08TT9VJMI1okcL/

19. Gabi Warwick. *Dayton man indicted in connection with shooting*
     death of his cousin. Fox45Now, 2018
     https://fox45now.com/news/local/dayton-man-indicted-for-shooting-
     death-of-his-cousin

20. DREESE, DUTTON, NEUMEIER, WILKEY. *A PEOPLE'S*
     HISTORY: TEACHING AN URBAN NEIGHBORHOOD AS A PLACE
     OF SOCIAL EMPOWERMENT. 2008
     https://blogs.miamioh.edu/cce-otr/files/2016/10/Teach-the-City.pdf

21. Paul Tough. *Helping Children Succeed, 2016.*

22. *Basic Statistics*, Talk Poverty, 2018. https://talkpoverty.org/basics/

23. Carlos Ballesteros, *ALABAMA HAS THE WORST POVERTY IN THE DEVELOPED WORLD, U.N. OFFICIAL SAYS.* Newsweek, 2017. http://www.newsweek.com/alabama-un-poverty-environmental-racism-743601

24. David Denby, *The Limits of Grit.* The New Yorker, 2016. https://www.newyorker.com/culture/culture-desk/the-limits-of-grit

25. Marc Dominic, *Here's how Flint went from boom town to nation's highest poverty rate*

26. *CNN Library. Flint Water Crisis Fast Facts,* CNN, 2018. http://www.cnn.com/2016/03/04/us/flint-water-crisis-fast-facts/

27. https://www.sentencingproject.org/criminal-justice-facts/

28. Meredith Crilly, *What are causes of fatigue during exercise?* LiveStrong. https://www.livestrong.com/article/380808-what-are-causes-of-fatigue-during-exercise/

29. Mayo Staff Clinic, *10 ways to control high blood pressure without medication.* Mayo Clinic, 2019. http://www.mayoclinic.org/diseases-conditions/high-blood-pressure/in-depth/high-blood-pressure/art-20046974

30. *Why This Town is Dying From Cancer.* AJ+, 2018.

31. https://www.cdc.gov/tobacco/data_statistics/fact_sheets/fast_facts/

32. https://en.wikipedia.org/wiki/Fight-or-flight_response

33. *Current Cigarette smoking among adults in the United States.* Centers for Disease Control and Prevention, 2017.

https://www.cdc.gov/tobacco/data_statistics/fact_sheets/adult_data/cig_smoking/

34.   Kim Ann Zimmerman. *Hurricane Katrina: Facts, Damage & Aftermath*, LIVE SCI=NCE, 2015

Author Biography

ShoMari Payne was born and raised in Dayton, Ohio. He was born into less than ideal circumstances and was raised in a house with deplorable conditions. He slept on the floor every night until the day he landed on the campus of Western Kentucky University by way of an ACT score. He overcame many barriers in route to becoming in an educator in Southwest Ohio, having worked as a Public-School Teacher, Academic Advisor, and Instructor for various colleges/schools in the area. ShoMari earned his B.S and M.S degrees from Western Kentucky University, and is in the process of completing his MBA at Miami University. ShoMari decided to share his experience of poverty and oppression in hopes of inspiring young men and women across the globe that they too can overcome insurmountable odds and create a better life for themselves.

Made in the USA
Lexington, KY
02 April 2019